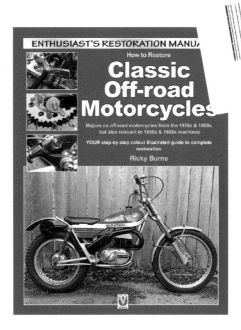

ENTHUSIAST'S RESTORATION MANUAL

How to Restore

Classic
Off-road
Motorcycles

Majors on off-road motorcycles from the 1970s & 1980s,
but also relevant to 1950s & 1960s machines

YOUR step-by-step colour illustrated guide to complete
restoration

Ricky Burns

Other great books from Veloce –

Speedpro Series
4-Cylinder Engine Short Block High-Performance Manual – New Updated & Revised Edition (Hammill)
Alfa Romeo DOHC High-performance Manual (Kartalamakis)
Alfa Romeo V6 Engine High-performance Manual (Kartalamakis)
BMC 998cc A-series Engine, How to Power Tune (Hammill)
1275cc A-series High-performance Manual (Hammill)
Camshafts – How to Choose & Time Them For Maximum Power (Hammill)
Competition Car Datalogging Manual, The (Templeman)
Cylinder Heads, How to Build, Modify & Power Tune – Updated & Revised Edition (Burgess & Gollan)
Distributor-type Ignition Systems, How to Build & Power Tune – New 3rd Edition (Hammill)
Fast Road Car, How to Plan and Build – Revised & Updated Colour New Edition (Stapleton)
Ford SOHC 'Pinto' & Sierra Cosworth DOHC Engines, How to Power Tune – Updated & Enlarged Edition (Hammill)
Ford V8, How to Power Tune Small Block Engines (Hammill)
Harley-Davidson Evolution Engines, How to Build & Power Tune (Hammill)
Holley Carburetors, How to Build & Power Tune – Revised & Updated Edition (Hammill)
Honda Civic Type R High-Performance Manual, The (Cowland & Clifford)
Jaguar XK Engines, How to Power Tune – Revised & Updated Colour Edition (Hammill)
Land Rover Discovery, Defender & Range Rover – How to Modify Coil Sprung Models for High Performance & Off-Road Action (Hosier)
MG Midget & Austin-Healey Sprite, How to Power Tune – New 3rd Edition (Stapleton)
MGB 4-cylinder Engine, How to Power Tune (Burgess)
MGB V8 Power, How to Give Your – Third Colour Edition (Williams)
MGB, MGC & MGB V8, How to Improve – New 2nd Edition (Williams)
Mini Engines, How to Power Tune On a Small Budget – Colour Edition (Hammill)
Motorcycle-engined Racing Car, How to Build (Pashley)
Motorsport, Getting Started in (Collins)
Nissan GT-R High-performance Manual, The (Gorodji)
Nitrous Oxide High-performance Manual, The (Langfield)
Race & Trackday Driving Techniques (Hornsey)
Retro or classic car for high performance, How to modify your (Stapleton)
Rover V8 Engines, How to Power Tune (Hammill)
Secrets of Speed – Today's techniques for 4-stroke engine blueprinting & tuning (Swager)
Sportscar & Kitcar Suspension & Brakes, How to Build & Modify – Revised 3rd Edition (Hammill)
SU Carburettor High-performance Manual (Hammill)
Successful Low-Cost Rally Car, How to Build a (Young)
Suzuki 4x4, How to Modify For Serious Off-road Action (Richardson)
Tiger Avon Sportscar, How to Build Your Own – Updated & Revised 2nd Edition (Dudley)
TR2, 3 & TR4, How to Improve (Williams)
TR5, 250 & TR6, How to Improve (Williams)
TR7 & TR8, How to Improve (Williams)
V8 Engine, How to Build a Short Block For High Performance (Hammill)
Volkswagen Beetle Suspension, Brakes & Chassis, How to Modify For High Performance (Hale)
Volkswagen Bus Suspension, Brakes & Chassis for High Performance, How to Modify – Updated & Enlarged New Edition (Hale)
Weber DCOE, & Dellorto DHLA Carburetors, How to Build & Power Tune – 3rd Edition (Hammill)

RAC handbooks
Caring for your car – How to maintain & service your car (Fry)
Caring for your car's bodywork and interior (Nixon)
Caring for your bicycle – How to maintain & repair your bicycle (Henshaw)
Caring for your scooter – How to maintain & service your 49cc to 125cc twist & go scooter (Fry)
Efficient Driver's Handbook, The (Moss)
Electric Cars – The Future is Now! (Linde)
First aid for your car – Your expert guide to common problems & how to fix them (Collins)
How your car works (Linde)
How your motorcycle works – Your guide to the components & systems of modern motorcycles (Henshaw)
Motorcycles – A first-time-buyer's guide (Henshaw)
Motorhomes – A first-time-buyer's guide (Fry)
Pass the MoT test! – How to check & prepare your car for the annual MoT test (Paxton)
Selling your car – How to make your car look great and how to sell it fast (Knight)
Simple fixes for your car – How to do small jobs for yourself and save money (Collins)

Enthusiast's Restoration Manual Series
Beginner's Guide to Classic Motorcycle Restoration YOUR step-by-step guide to setting up a workshop, choosing a project, dismantling, sourcing parts, renovating & rebuilding classic motorcycles from the 1970s & 1980s, The (Burns)
Citroën 2CV, How to Restore (Porter)
Classic Large Frame Vespa Scooters, How to Restore (Paxton)
Classic Car Bodywork, How to Restore (Thaddeus)
Classic British Car Electrical Systems (Astley)
Classic Car Electrics (Thaddeus)
Classic Cars, How to Paint (Thaddeus)
Ducati Bevel Twins 1971 to 1986 (Falloon)
How to restore Honda CX500 & CX650 – YOUR step-by-step colour illustrated guide to complete restoration (Burns)
How to restore Honda Fours – YOUR step-by-step colour illustrated guide to complete restoration (Burns)
Jaguar E-type (Crespin)
Reliant Regal, How to Restore (Payne)
Triumph TR2, 3, 3A, 4 & 4A, How to Restore (Williams)
Triumph TR5/250 & 6, How to Restore (Williams)
Triumph TR7/8, How to Restore (Williams)
Triumph Trident T150/T160 & BSA Rocket III, How to Restore (Rooke)
Ultimate Mini Restoration Manual, The (Ayre & Webber)
Volkswagen Beetle, How to Restore (Tyler)
VW Bay Window Bus (Paxton)
Yamaha FS1-E, How to Restore (Watts)

Expert Guides
Land Rover Series I-III – Your expert guide to common problems & how to fix them (Thurman)
MG Midget & A-H Sprite – Your expert guide to common problems & how to fix them (Horler)

Essential Buyer's Guide Series
Triumph Herald & Vitesse (Davies)
Triumph Spitfire & GT6 (Baugues)
Triumph Stag (Mort)
Triumph Thunderbird, Trophy & Tiger (Henshaw)
Triumph TR6 (Williams)
Triumph TR7 & TR8 (Williams)

Great Cars
Austin-Healey – A celebration of the fabulous 'Big' Healey (Piggott)
Triumph TR - TR2 to 6: The last of the traditional sports cars (Piggott)

General
1½-litre GP Racing 1961-1965 (Whitelock)
AC Two-litre Saloons & Buckland Sportscars (Archibald)
Alfa Romeo 155/156/147 Competition Touring Cars (Collins)
Alfa Romeo Giulia Coupé GT & GTA (Tipler)
Alfa Romeo Montreal – The dream car that came true (Taylor)
Alfa Romeo Montreal – The Essential Companion (Classic Reprint of 500 copies) (Taylor)
Alfa Tipo 33 (McDonough & Collins)
Alpine & Renault – The Development of the Revolutionary Turbo F1 Car 1968 to 1979 (Smith)
Alpine & Renault – The Sports Prototypes 1963 to 1969 (Smith)
Alpine & Renault – The Sports Prototypes 1973 to 1978 (Smith)
Anatomy of the Classic Mini (Huthert & Ely)
Anatomy of the Works Minis (Moylan)
Armstrong-Siddeley (Smith)
Art Deco and British Car Design (Down)
Autodrome (Collins & Ireland)
Autodrome 2 (Collins & Ireland)
Automotive A-Z, Lane's Dictionary of Automotive Terms (Lane)
Automotive Mascots (Kay & Springate)
Bahamas Speed Weeks, The (O'Neil)
Bentley Continental, Corniche and Azure (Bennett)
Bentley MkVI, Rolls-Royce Silver Wraith, Dawn & Cloud/Bentley R & S-Series (Nutland)
Bluebird CN7 (Stevens)
BMC Competitions Department Secrets (Turner, Chambers & Browning)
BMW 5-Series (Cranswick)
BMW Z-Cars (Taylor)
BMW Boxer Twins 1970-1995 Bible, The (Falloon)
BMW Cafe Racers (Cloesen)
BMW Custom Motorcycles – Choppers, Cruisers, Bobbers, Trikes & Quads (Cloesen)
BMW – The Power of M (Vivian)
Bonjour – Is this Italy? (Turner)
British 250cc Racing Motorcycles (Pereira)
British at Indianapolis, The (Wagstaff)
British Café Racers (Cloesen)
British Cars, The Complete Catalogue of, 1895-1975 (Culshaw & Horrobin)
British Custom Motorcycles – The Brit Chop – choppers, cruisers, bobbers & trikes (Cloesen)
BRM – A Mechanic's Tale (Salmon)
BRM V16 (Ludvigsen)
BSA Bantam Bible, The (Henshaw)
BSA Motorcycles – the final evolution (Jones)
Bugatti Type 40 (Price)
Bugatti 46/50 Updated Edition (Price & Arbey)
Bugatti T44 & T49 (Price & Arbey)
Bugatti 57 2nd Edition (Price)
Bugatti Type 57 Grand Prix – A Celebration (Tomlinson)
Caravan, Improve & Modify Your (Porter)
Caravans, The Illustrated History 1919-1959 (Jenkinson)
Caravans, The Illustrated History From 1960 (Jenkinson)
Carrera Panamericana, La (Tipler)
Chrysler 300 – America's Most Powerful Car 2nd Edition (Ackerson)
Chrysler PT Cruiser (Ackerson)
Citroën DS (Bobbitt)
Classic British Car Electrical Systems (Astley)
Cobra – The Real Thing! (Legate)
Competition Car Aerodynamics 3rd Edition (McBeath)
Competition Car Composites A Practical Handbook (Revised 2nd Edition) (McBeath)
Concept Cars, How to illustrate and design (Dewey)
Cortina – Ford's Bestseller (Robson)
Coventry Climax Racing Engines (Hammill)
Daily Mirror 1970 World Cup Rally 40, The (Robson)
Daimler SP250 New Edition (Long)
Datsun Fairlady Roadster to 280ZX – The Z-Car Story (Long)
Dino – The V6 Ferrari (Long)
Dodge Challenger & Plymouth Barracuda (Grist)
Dodge Charger – Enduring Thunder (Ackerson)
Dodge Dynamite! (Grist)
Dorset from the Sea – The Jurassic Coast from Lyme Regis to Old Harry Rocks photographed from its best viewpoint (Belasco)
Dorset from the Sea – The Jurassic Coast from Lyme Regis to Old Harry Rocks photographed from its best viewpoint (souvenir edition) (Belasco)
Draw & Paint Cars – How to (Gardiner)
Drive on the Wild Side, A – 20 Extreme Driving Adventures From Around the World (Weaver)
Ducati 750 Bible, The (Falloon)
Ducati 750 SS 'round-case' 1974, The Book of the (Falloon)
Ducati 860, 900 and Mille Bible, The (Falloon)
Ducati Monster Bible (New Updated & Revised Edition), The (Falloon)
Ducati 916 (updated edition) (Falloon)
Dune Buggy, Building A – The Essential Manual (Shakespeare)
Dune Buggy Files (Hale)
Dune Buggy Handbook (Hale)
East German Motor Vehicles in Pictures (Suhr/Weinreich)
Fast Ladies – Female Racing Drivers 1888 to 1970 (Bouzanquet)
Fate of the Sleeping Beauties, The (op de Weegh/Hottendorff/op de Weegh)
Ferrari 288 GTO, The Book of the (Sackey)
Ferrari 333 SP (O'Neil)
Fiat & Abarth 124 Spider & Coupé (Tipler)
Fiat & Abarth 500 & 600 – 2nd Edition (Bobbitt)
Fiats, Great Small (Ward)
Fine Art of the Motorcycle Engine, The (Peirce)
Ford Cleveland 335-Series V8 engine 1970 to 1982 – The Essential Source Book (Hammill)
Ford F100/F150 Pick-up 1948-1996 (Ackerson)
Ford F150 Pick-up 1997-2005 (Ackerson)
Ford GT – Then, and Now (Streather)
Ford GT40 (Legate)
Ford Midsize Muscle – Fairlane, Torino & Ranchero (Cranswick)
Ford Model Y (Roberts)
Ford Small Block V8 Racing Engines 1962-1970 – The Essential Source Book (Hammill)
Ford Thunderbird From 1954, The Book of the (Long)
Formula 5000 Motor Racing, Back then ... and back now (Lawson)
Forza Minardi! (Vigar)
France: the essential guide for car enthusiasts – 200 things for the car enthusiast to see and do (Parish)
From Crystal Palace to Red Square – A Hapless Biker's Road to Russia (Turner)
Funky Mopeds (Skelton)
Grand Prix Ferrari – The Years of Enzo Ferrari's Power, 1948-1980 (Pritchard)
Grand Prix Ford – DFV-powered Formula 1 Cars (Robson)
GT – The World's Best GT Cars 1953-73 (Dawson)
Hillclimbing & Sprinting – The Essential Manual (Short & Wilkinson)
Honda NSX (Long)
Inside the Rolls-Royce & Bentley Styling Department – 1971 to 2001 (Hull)
Intermeccanica – The Story of the Prancing Bull (McCredie & Reisner)
Italian Cafe Racers (Cloesen)
Italian Custom Motorcycles (Cloesen)
Jaguar, The Rise of (Price)
Jaguar XJ 220 – The Inside Story (Moreton)
Jaguar XJ-S, The Book of the (Long)
Jeep CJ (Ackerson)
Jeep Wrangler (Ackerson)
The Jowett Jupiter - The car that leaped to fame (Nankivell)
Karmann-Ghia Coupé & Convertible (Bobbitt)
Kawasaki Triples Bible, The (Walker)
Kawasaki Z1 Story, The (Sheehan)
Kris Meeke – Intercontinental Rally Challenge Champion (McBride)
Lamborghini Miura Bible, The (Sackey)
Lamborghini Urraco, The Book of the (Landsem)
Lambretta Bible, The (Davies)
Lancia 037 (Collins)
Lancia Delta HF Integrale (Blaettel & Wagner)
Land Rover Series III Reborn (Porter)
Land Rover, The Half-ton Military (Cook)
Laverda Twins & Triples Bible 1968-1986 (Falloon)
Lea-Francis Story, The (Price)
Le Mans Panoramic (Ireland)
Lexus Story, The (Long)
Little book of microcars, the (Quellin)
Little book of smart, the – New Edition (Jackson)
Little book of trikes, the (Quellin)
Lola – The Illustrated History (1957-1977) (Starkey)
Lola – All the Sports Racing & Single-seater Racing Cars 1978-1997 (Starkey)
Lola T70 – The Racing History & Individual Chassis Record – 4th Edition (Starkey)
Lotus 18 Colin Chapman's U-turn (Whitelock)
Lotus 49 (Oliver)
Marketingmobiles, The Wonderful Wacky World of (Hale)
Maserati 250F In Focus (Pritchard)
Mazda MX-5/Miata 1.6 Enthusiast's Workshop Manual (Grainger & Shoemark)
Mazda MX-5/Miata 1.8 Enthusiast's Workshop Manual (Grainger & Shoemark)
Mazda MX-5 Miata, The book of the – The 'Mk1' NA-series 1988 to 1997 (Long)
Mazda MX-5 Miata Roadster (Long)
Mazda Rotary-engined Cars (Cranshaw)
Maximum Mini (Booij)
Meet the English (Bowie)
Mercedes-Benz SL – R230 series 2001 to 2011 (Long)
Mercedes-Benz SL – W113-series 1963-1971 (Long)
Mercedes-Benz SL & SLC – 107-series 1971-1989 (Long)
Mercedes-Benz SLK – R170 series 1996-2004 (Long)
Mercedes-Benz SLK – R171 series 2004-2011 (Long)
Mercedes-Benz W123-series – All models 1976 to 1986 (Long)
Mercedes G-Wagen (Long)
MGA (Price Williams)
MGB & MGB GT– Expert Guide (Auto-doc Series) (Williams)
MGB Electrical Systems Updated & Revised Edition (Astley)
Micro Caravans (Jenkinson)
Micro Trucks (Mort)
Microcars at Large! (Quellin)
Mini Cooper – The Real Thing! (Tipler)
Mini Minor to Asia Minor (West)
Mitsubishi Lancer Evo, The Road Car & WRC Story (Long)
Montlhéry, The Story of the Paris Autodrome (Boddy)
Morgan Maverick (Lawrence)
Morgan 3 Wheeler – back to the future!, The (Dron)
Morris Minor, 60 Years on the Road (Newell)
Moto Guzzi Sport & Le Mans Bible, The (Falloon)
Motor Movies – The Posters! (Veysey)
Motor Racing – Reflections of a Lost Era (Carter)
Motor Racing – The Pursuit of Victory 1930-1962 (Carter)
Motor Racing – The Pursuit of Victory 1963-1972 (Wyatt/Sears)
Motor Racing Heroes – The Stories of 100 Greats (Newman)
Motorcycle Apprentice (Cakebread)
Motorcycle GP Racing in the 1960s (Pereira)
Motorcycle Road & Racing Chassis Designs (Noakes)
Motorhomes, The Illustrated History (Jenkinson)
Motorsport In colour, 1950s (Wainwright)
MV Agusta Fours, The book of the classic (Falloon)
N.A.R.T. – A concise history of the North American Racing Team 1957 to 1983 (O'Neil)
Nissan 300ZX & 350Z – The Z-Car Story (Long)
Nissan GT-R Supercar: Born to race (Gorodji)
Northeast American Sports Car Races 1950-1959 (O'Neil)
Nothing Runs – Misadventures in the Classic, Collectable & Exotic Car Biz (Slutsky)
Off-Road Giants! (Volume 1) – Heroes of 1960s Motorcycle Sport (Westlake)
Off-Road Giants! (Volume 2) – Heroes of 1960s Motorcycle Sport (Westlake)
Off-Road Giants! (volume 3) – Heroes of 1960s Motorcycle Sport (Westlake)
Pass the Theory and Practical Driving Tests (Gibson & Hoole)
Peking to Paris 2007 (Young)
Pontiac Firebird (Cranswick)
Porsche Boxster (Long)
Porsche 356 (2nd Edition) (Long)
Porsche 908 (Födisch, Neßhöver, Roßbach, Schwarz & Roßbach)
Porsche 911 Carrera – The Last of the Evolution (Corlett)
Porsche 911R, RS & RSR, 4th Edition (Starkey)
Porsche 911, The Book of the (Long)
Porsche 911 – The Definitive History 2004-2012 (Long)
Porsche – The Racing 914s (Smith)
Porsche 911SC 'Super Carrera' – The Essential Companion (Streather)
Porsche 914 & 914-6: The Definitive History of the Road & Competition Cars (Long)
Porsche 924 (Long)
The Porsche 924 Carreras – evolution to excellence (Smith)
Porsche 928 (Long)
Porsche 944 (Long)
Porsche 964, 993 & 996 Data Plate Code Breaker (Streather)
Porsche 993 'King Of Porsche' – The Essential Companion (Streather)
Porsche 996 'Supreme Porsche' – The Essential Companion (Streather)
Porsche 997 2004-2012 – Porsche Excellence (Streather)
Porsche Racing Cars – 1953 to 1975 (Long)
Porsche Racing Cars – 1976 to 2005 (Long)
Porsche – The Rally Story (Meredith)
Porsche: Three Generations of Genius (Meredith)
Preston Tucker & Others (Linde)
RAC Rally Action! (Gardiner)
RACING COLOURS – MOTOR RACING COMPOSITIONS 1908-2009 (Newman)
Racing Line – British motorcycle racing in the golden age of the big single (Guntrip)
Rallye Sport Fords: The Inside Story (Moreton)
Renewable Energy Home Handbook, The (Porter)
Roads with a View – England's greatest views and how to find them by road (Corfield)
Rolls-Royce Silver Shadow/Bentley T Series Corniche & Camargue – Revised & Enlarged Edition (Bobbitt)
Rolls-Royce Silver Spirit, Silver Spur & Bentley Mulsanne 2nd Edition (Bobbitt)
Rover P4 (Bobbitt)
Runways & Racers (O'Neil)
Russian Motor Vehicles – Soviet Limousines 1930-2003 (Kelly)
Russian Motor Vehicles – The Czarist Period 1784 to 1917 (Kelly)
RX-7 – Mazda's Rotary Engine Sportscar (Updated & Revised New Edition) (Long)
Scooters & Microcars, The A-Z of Popular (Dan)
Scooter Lifestyle (Grainger)
SCOOTER MANIA! – Recollections of the Isle of Man International Scooter Rally (Jackson)
Singer Story: Cars, Commercial Vehicles, Bicycles & Motorcycle (Atkinson)
Sleeping Beauties USA – abandoned classic cars & trucks (Marek)
SM – Citroën's Maserati-engined Supercar (Long & Claverol)
Speedway – Auto racing's ghost tracks (Collins & Ireland)
Sprite Caravans, The Story of (Jenkinson)
Standard Motor Company, The Book of the (Robson)
Steve Hole's Kit Car Cornucopia – Cars, Companies, Stories, Facts & Figures: the UK's kit car scene since 1949 (Hole)
Subaru Impreza: The Road Car And WRC Story (Long)
Supercar, How to Build your own (Thompson)
Tales from the Toolbox (Oliver)
Tatra – The Legacy of Hans Ledwinka, Updated & Enlarged Collector's Edition of 1500 copies (Margolius & Henry)
Taxi! The Story of the 'London' Taxicab (Bobbitt)
Toleman Story, The (Hilton)
Toyota Celica & Supra, The Book of Toyota's Sports Coupés (Long)
Toyota MR2 Coupés & Spyders (Long)
Triumph Bonneville Bible (59-83) (Henshaw)
Triumph Bonneville!, Save the – The inside story of the Meriden Workers' Co-op (Rosamond)
Triumph Motorcycles & the Meriden Factory (Hancox)
Triumph Speed Twin & Thunderbird Bible (Woolridge)
Triumph Tiger Cub Bible (Estall)
Triumph Trophy Bible (Woolridge)
Triumph TR6 (Kimberley)
TT Talking – The TT's most exciting era – As seen by Manx Radio TT's lead commentator 2004-2012 (Lambert)
Two Summers – The Mercedes-Benz W196R Racing Car (Ackerson)
TWR Story, The – Group A (Hughes & Scott)
Unraced (Collins)
Velocette Motorcycles – MSS to Thruxton – New Third Edition (Burris)
Vespa – The Story of a Cult Classic in Pictures (Uhlig)
Vincent Motorcycles: The Untold Story since 1946 (Guyony & Parker)
Volkswagen Bus Book, The (Bobbitt)
Volkswagen Bus or Van to Camper, How to Convert (Porter)
Volkswagens of the World (Glen)
VW Beetle Cabriolet – The full story of the convertible Beetle (Bobbitt)
VW Beetle – The Car of the 20th Century (Copping)
VW Bus – 40 Years of Splitties, Bays & Wedges (Copping)
VW Bus Book, The (Bobbitt)
VW Golf: Five Generations of Fun (Copping & Cservenka)
VW – The Air-cooled Era (Copping)
VW T5 Camper Conversion Manual (Porter)
VW Campers (Copping)
You & Your Jaguar XK8/XKR – Buying, Enjoying, Maintaining, Modifying – New Edition (Thorley)
Which Oil? – Choosing the right oils & greases for your antique, vintage, veteran, classic or collector car (Michell)
Works Minis, The Last (Purves & Brenchley)
Works Rally Mechanic (Moylan)

For post publication news, updates and amendments relating to this book please visit www.veloce.co.uk/books/V4950

www.veloce.co.uk

First published February 2017 by Veloce Publishing Limited, Veloce House, Parkway Farm Business Park, Middle Farm Way, Poundbury, Dorchester, Dorset, DT1 3AR, England. Fax 01305 250479/e-mail info@veloce.co.uk/ web www.veloce.co.uk or www.velocebooks.com.
ISBN: 978-1-845849-50-4 UPC: 6-36847-04950-8

© Ricky Burns and Veloce Publishing 2017. All rights reserved. With the exception of quoting brief passages for the purpose of review, no part of this publication may be recorded, reproduced or transmitted by any means, including photocopying, without the written permission of Veloce Publishing Ltd. Throughout this book logos, model names and designations, etc, have been used for the purposes of identification, illustration and decoration. Such names are the property of the trademark holder as this is not an official publication.

Readers with ideas for automotive books, or books on other transport or related hobby subjects, are invited to write to the editorial director of Veloce Publishing at the above address.
British Library Cataloguing in Publication Data – A catalogue record for this book is available from the British Library.
Typesetting, design and page make-up all by Veloce Publishing Ltd on Apple Mac. Printed in India by Replika Press.

ENTHUSIAST'S RESTORATION MANUAL™

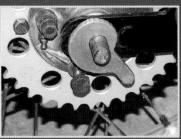

How to Restore

Classic Off-road Motorcycles

Majors on off-road motorcycles from the 1970s & 1980s, but also relevant to 1950s & 1960s machines

YOUR step-by-step colour illustrated guide to complete restoration

Ricky Burns

Veloce

Contents

Introduction

Like many riders, my first experience of motorcycles came when I was far too young to ride legally on the public roads. I took to riding in local fields and woodland – anywhere where there was open space and relatively few people. At first, I used a crudely converted road bike of very limited engine size, a Honda SS90, as I remember, with knobbly tyres fitted and as much road kit as possible removed.

I had great fun, and have fond memories of that little Honda, but time passed, and then, through *Trials and Motocross* news, I discovered what real off-road bikes were. I visited as many scramble events as I could, and eventually managed to convince my father to buy me a scrambler. My first real scrambler was a Greeves Challenger; even then it looked old-fashioned to me, but boy did it go! Living close to the Greeves factory, in Thundersley, England, made this a good choice, because we always seemed to need one part or another to keep it going.

After a while, I exchanged the Greeves for an almost-new Suzuki TM250 – much more modern than the Greeves, but still not ideal: the local fields were a little too close to my neighbours and we often got complaints about the noise.

A friend of mine had a Bultaco trials bike, which was almost silent compared to my Suzuki; he never had complaints from our neighbours. So I visited several trials events and decided to trade in my Suzuki for a trials bike: I wanted to continue

A Suzuki TM250 scrambler similar to the one I owned in my early teens.

riding, but I also wanted to keep my neighbours happy. That was the beginning of many years of off-road riding that I still do today.

Numerous clubs worldwide that hold specific events for classic off-road machines, and countless older competition motorcycles are out still there waiting to be restored and used again. Some models now fetch a premium figure when they come up for sale, particularly if they were very competitive at the time.

Those days of early off-road riding have never left me and I have maintained a keen interest in competition bikes of that period.

How to Restore Classic Off-road Motorcycles is applicable to models as varied as a Maico Scrambler or a Pre '65 BSA trials bike – the restoration process is the same, despite the differences in the way they work.

The example used in this book is a Spanish trials bike, since they dominated off-road competition for a good period of time; in this instance, a 1979 Montesa Cota 349. However, this could have been just about any trials, motocross (scramble) or Enduro bike of the same period, given that the vast majority were single cylinder machines.

This book provides a step-by-step guide from choosing your project, through the complete strip down, rebuild, right up to the first start-up and ride. Because this book is primarily a guide to restoration and covers restoration techniques, it is recommended to be used in conjunction with the appropriate workshop manual for your model.

VISIT VELOCE ON THE WEB – WWW.VELOCE.CO.UK
All current books • New book news • Special offers • Gift vouchers • Forum

7

Chapter 1
Project assessment

Inevitably, off-road bikes lead a harder life than standard road bikes, but they're built to endure the rigours of off-road competition, and should prove reliable if correctly maintained; if not, they'll fall into disrepair very quickly. Often cables are not adjusted properly, leading to clutch/gearbox problems; or chain and sprockets are not lubricated, leading to premature wear. General misuse or bad handling when loading or unloading from a van leads to unnecessary damage to mudguards (fenders) and fuel tanks, etc. Then there's the competition itself: bikes are often dropped and crashed during an event, so bent or broken levers and twisted forks are common problems.

The classic off-road motorcycles for sale these days generally fall into two categories. First, those in great condition and well-maintained, either original or restored (generally advertised at relatively high prices); and second, those that may have recently been rediscovered after years of neglect (often found by someone who has no knowledge of motorcycles and is simply selling to make room or a fast buck). If you're looking for a restoration project, you'll be buying something that falls into this second category. With more and more trials, motocross and enduro classes being added all the time, there's an event for every model you're likely to find.

1.1 A pristine example of a 1956 BSA Gold Star trials bike, commanding a hefty sum.

1.2 A typical off-roader in poor condition, needing restoration. This one's almost complete, with only a few parts missing, making it a viable project.

There are plenty of restoration projects available, so don't jump at the first one that you see – unless, of course, after reading this chapter, the project that you have found ticks all the right boxes.

While on the subject of boxes, I would say right now that if you come across a project that's in boxes, walk away. The chances are the boxes contain all the major parts needed for a restoration, but it's not the major parts that are difficult to find – it's the smaller parts, the parts that are low cost and easily lost if separated from the bike: because they're low value, they're never advertised for sale.

Try to buy a complete bike; even one in poor condition will have all those little parts required, and, as you start to strip down, you can box them up and save them for later when you're rebuilding. I have learnt the project-in-a-box lesson the hard way and I would never do it again.

Whether you already have your bike or are about to buy one, it's always a good idea to set out a rebuild plan. To do this, you'll need to carry out a project assessment. Once this has been done, you'll have a better understanding of the work and cost involved in your restoration.

So what are you up against? It's possible that the engine has seized through lack of use. This can

sometimes be solved with a little patience over a few weeks by pouring a little oil into the cylinder and letting it soak. If you are lucky the oil will work its way in between the piston and the cylinder walls, and help to free the piston. But in most cases, you'll need to remove the engine and carry out at least a partial rebuild. You already know that parts are missing,

and they may be hard to come by now – particularly engine parts. The paintwork will have deteriorated, as will chrome plating or polished alloy. Once a bike has been left standing, parts begin to seize, rubber begins to crack, and chrome and alloy oxidise. You'll need to assess what the original problem was and fix it during your restoration. For us enthusiasts this is all part of the fun, isn't it? Well it is for me.

Many of the faults set out below are normal on most projects, so don't be concerned if your bike has some of these defects – after all, it's a restoration project. If you know what to look out for, it'll help you decide if this is the right project for you, and act as a bargaining tool when negotiating a price with the seller.

Make a checklist for when you first view your project. Almost all problems can be overcome, but the worse it is, the more expensive it'll be to rectify.

FIRST IMPRESSIONS
Start with your overall first impression of the motorcycle. Is it all there? Are there obviously parts missing? Chain tensioner, levers, and – if the model was registered for road use – the original lighting kit, are common missing parts.

1.3 On initial inspection, this engine looks very neglected.

1.4 Here, we have an engine mounting bolt with a nut missing – it didn't say that in the advert!

1.5 Off-road damage: a cracked and badly-scratched rear mudguard (fender).

Lots of trials and enduro bikes would have been road registered, so are the documents present? The correct documentation will save you time, when trying to make the bike road legal again.

Does the owner have old manuals? Many do, and it's a real bonus if they come with the bike. Online forums have digital manuals now, but a hard copy is good to have.

Are there spare parts? An owner may have a box full of bits that they think are worthless; take them if they're available – often you'll find a part that is required later on.

Does it look as though someone just stopped using it and left it as it was the last time it was ridden, or does it appear to have been tinkered with? Giveaway signs are bolts and screws or small parts missing.

BASIC ENGINE ASSESSMENT
Now let's begin with a basic engine check. Before attempting to start an engine, make sure it has engine and or two-stroke oil of the correct fuel:oil ratio – this can be found in the owner's manual. If there's no manual available, an internet forum is a good place to find this information.

If it starts and runs, great. Look out for excessive smoke, rattles, etc. If your model has a two-stroke engine, it will smoke on first start-up. It will be rich with the choke on, and may look a little smoky until warmed up. Once it has, there should still be some light smoke. Don't confuse smoke with steam. If a bike had been unused for some time, moisture can build up in the exhaust and will turn to steam on start-up. Smoke will be darker, with a more oily smell. If your model is a four-stroke, however, you should not see any smoke from the exhaust, once the engine has warmed up.

Are there unusual noises? Listen out for internal knocking or rattles. A little noise may be present at first, but the engine should quieten once it has warmed up and the choke has been turned off.

Some engines rattle a little if they're not set at the correct tickover speed, but it's quite common on a competition bike not to have a tickover set at all, for safety reasons, so that, if you suffer a fall while riding, the engine cuts out right away. Bring

1.6 Check that the spline shafts on gears and kickstart are good, like the one above. I've seen gearlevers welded to the shaft: an awful 'repair' which can only be rectified properly if a replacement shaft is available.

1.7 The spline on this kickstart lever has worn beyond repair, and a new kickstart lever is needed.

1.8 Broken clutch plates.

the revs up to around 1500rpm to listen to the engine at a running speed: it should now run smoothly, with no unusual noises. If you're unfamiliar with how an engine should sound, take a friend with you who has more experience in these matters; or try to attend a competition meeting, where you will hear first hand what the engine should sound like.

If the engine does not start
Does the engine turn over? Gently try the kickstart to see if it does. This will tell you if the engine's seized. A seized engine can be expensive to resolve, but not always. (If you go ahead and purchase the bike, smear some light oil on the sparkplug hole and leave for a day or two for it to penetrate scale. Then gently try again, but do not force it.)

Is the sparkplug missing? It's not a good sign – especially if the bike's stored outside – to have a missing sparkplug. Moisture will have got in and led to cylinder damage. I had to buy a complete cylinder head for a Honda once, because water had corroded the head behind a valve seat – all because someone had left a sparkplug out. If you have a two-stroke, you'll not encounter valve problems. But still be wary if the sparkplugs have been left out for years.

Can you pull in the clutch lever and open the throttle smoothly? This'll give you an idea how long a bike has been standing. These take a long time to seize, and, if they're stuck, it's another problem that needs solving.

Can you select all the gears? Try rocking the bike backward and forward, while moving the gearlever to select all the gears. You may need help with this, if you find the bike heavy.

THE TANK AND SEAT
Checking the fuel tank

It's not easy to find a good secondhand fuel tank, and those that are available have a high asking price. Aftermarket fuel tanks are available for some models, particularly Pre '65 models, that often use alloy tanks.

Take a good look at the tank: cosmetic damage can be rectified; it's holes that you're really looking for. Remove the fuel cap and have a good look inside. Is it clean or dirty? How bad is it? If it has holes, it's very likely that you'll need another tank, although smaller holes (1-2mm) can be repaired.

1.9 This tank has rusted completely, leaving a large hole …

1.10 … this one looks much better inside, and should not present too many problems.

Does the tank have its shape? No bad dents or damage? Although this can be rectified, the worse it is, the more expensive it'll be to repair.

Checking the seat

In many cases, the seat cover's still intact. Cosmetic damage is easily dealt with: new covers are readily available. Make sure that the frame and seat base are in good condition. Check whether all the seat rubbers are still in place: if not, new seat rubbers are available.

Most early models have a metal seat base, prone to rust. A little rust can be dealt with, but a badly corroded seat base will need changing, if you can find one. If the seat base has corroded, there'll be nothing to attach the seat cover to, and you could have a problem securing the seat to the frame.

The foam is not such a problem, although it's a great advantage if your foam's in good shape. Cutting foam to shape is an art and not easy to get right, but minor repairs are quite easy to deal with. Seat foam is available for many models.

1.11 Poor paintwork and missing decals can cost a considerable sum to resolve.

1.12 Bubbles and blisters could just be the paint peeling, but could also be a sign of fibreglass problems on this tank.

1.13 The seat cover is split, and will need to be replaced.

FRAME AND FORKS

Look for obvious damage to the frame and forks. A bike may have been in an accident, and a badly accident-damaged one should be avoided. Look out for bent forks, swinging arm, stands, footrests, gear and brake levers; dents; and deep scratches.

Take a look head on and from behind the bike to see if it looks square and symmetrical: footrests should be the same height and level with each other. Look at the exhaust pipes – the first part of the bike to be damaged if it falls over, but they're easily replaced, so can conceal an accident. Check the steering head, I found one to be almost oval in shape due to a heavy accident; it should, of course, be perfectly round.

The forks should be 100 per cent straight. It's an expensive job to replace stanchions and fork legs. Make sure you look at them properly, and compare them with each other. Check carefully that they're not bent.

The forks may have twisted round in the top and bottom yoke, so do not confuse this with being bent. Forks that are twisted can easily be reset, by loosening the top and bottom yoke bolts and pulling the forks straight.

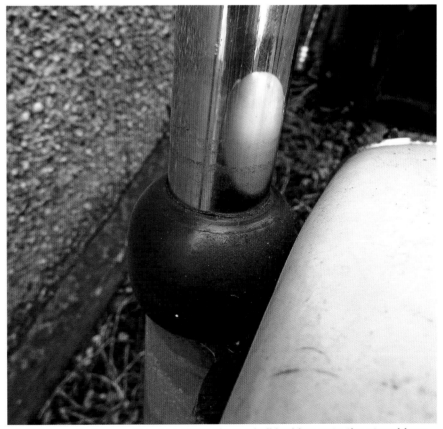

1.14 These forks are showing slight signs of oil leaking onto the stanchions. If the pitting is not within the lower fork leg range of movement, it's possible to leave regrinding until a later date. However it's recommended that the fork legs be re-chromed if possible.

1.15 This fork leg needs a good polish.

Take a look at the fork stanchions: if they're rusted and pitted, particularly lower down the stanchion, it's likely they'll need re-chroming. Some light rust can polish out, but anything other than this will lead to leaking oil seals. This is not uncommon, and, in most cases, the oil seals would be changed during a restoration.

It's normal for a bike that has been standing for some time to be low, if not empty, of fork oil. Push the forks down and let go quickly, does it bounce up and down quickly? The oil dampens the movement, so there should be very little bounce. If there's bounce, this shows that the damping has been lost, and it's likely that the seals will need replacing and the forks refilling with fork oil.

SPARES AVAILABILITY
Spares availability is good for most of the better known models, with an active cottage industry supplying parts that keep these bikes running. In fact, for some models you can even buy a complete new frame. Also, for earlier bikes, more modern parts, such as electronic ignition and belts to replace primary chains, are available. There are numerous companies that specialise in specific models, and there's a huge parts supply for a good range of models.

Some models shared parts with other bike of the same year, with many early two-stroke models using a Villers engine. This is a great help – as long as you know which model has the same parts as your bike, and gives you a much better chance of

finding a good condition used part, if originals are no longer available.

There is also a wide range aftermarket replica parts available. Some restorers do not like to use non-original parts; others do not mind so much, and there are some very good replica parts available that look almost identical to the original. Many parts, such as mudguards (fenders) and levers, are universal.

This is a list of parts that I would expect to change or buy on virtually every restoration:

- Piston rings, maybe with a re-bore and new pistons
- Clutch plates – not expensive
- Sparkplugs – always worn
- Contact breaker points – always worn
- Top end gasket set
- Carburettor rebuild kit – original falls apart when stripping carbs
- Front and rear brake shoes
- Tyres – always perished
- Inner tubes and rim tape
- Chain and sprocket set – chain always rusted solid, sprocket mostly worn
- Seat cover – almost always torn
- Spray paint, including primer filler and abrasive paper.
- Decal kit for tank after spraying
- Decal sticker set for frame and side panels, where appropriate.
- Oil
- Air filter
- Rubber fuel hoses

Couple this list with the parts that you know are missing, and you'll have a fair idea of the cost of parts that you'll need to buy. The rest is just work, and lots of it, but it's worth in the end, believe me.

VISIT VELOCE ON THE WEB – WWW.VELOCE.CO.UK
All current books • New book news • Special offers • Gift vouchers • Forum

14

Chapter 2
Sourcing parts

Sourcing parts for many off-road models is surprisingly easy, despite the age of some still competing today.

Small manufacturers are still producing new parts, some identical to the original part, others produced as an upgrade to the original that was unavailable years ago. There is also a wide range of parts that can be described as universal: items such as levers, mudguards, etc.

Once you have bought your first project, and begun the initial strip down, you'll quickly build up a large list of parts that you'll need. This list will grow the further you get into your restoration. There are a variety of sources for these parts.

THE INTERNET
The internet is undoubtedly the best place to start looking. eBay, for example, has thousands of parts advertised, from all over the world, and you'll often find at least half a dozen sellers offering the parts that you're looking for, with delivery only taking a few days.

Close-up photos give a good indication of the condition; though vague descriptions and blurry images aren't uncommon; be wary when ordering this way.

eBay's rule at the moment is that if you buy something on auction (not 'buy it now'), you have no right to a refund if you change your mind after the purchase, unless it was not as described be the seller. If the item you bought was a 'buy it now' instant purchase, then you have the option to ask the seller for a full refund if you find the part unsuitable; this normally includes your postage costs, too.

Be aware that, if you buy a part from an international seller, it's possible that you could be charged an import duty/tax, too! All countries have different import rules: check these before buying from an international seller.

Of course, the downside of buying from an internet seller is that, at the time of purchase, you can't actually see the item, and you'll have to wait for delivery before you can make a true assessment of its condition.

I live in the UK, and have purchased parts from USA, Germany, France, Japan and Hong Kong, and I have always been happy with what I have bought.

CLUBS AND FORUMS
The benefits of joining a club or forum cannot be emphasised enough. These are great for sourcing the parts you need, and by joining one, you'll get to know the best and recommended sources of parts for your bike.

Lots of existing members are marque specialists, who'll have owned and worked on their bikes for years. Between them, they'll have detailed knowledge of every single model and part, and give valued advice to new members – not only in regard to sourcing parts, but also in fault diagnosis, and explaining the easiest way to overcome a problem. You can be sure that members have come across the same problems that you're likely to face, and already know the simplest solution.

You'll find most forums that you visit have sections as follows:

- Faults and cures
- Meetings and events
- Restoration stories
- Buy, sell, exchange
- Recommended services
- Like for like items and good value eBay items

- Reference pictures of restored bikes and technical data
- Specials – modifications, aftermarket parts
- General chat

You can see by the subject list that there is very little, if anything, that isn't included. The references and tech help posts are very good, and the advice given will save you time and money while restoring your bike. There are forums and clubs for almost every motorcycle, and, for more common motorcycles, there are often several clubs or forums to better suit your needs.

Some forums and clubs even have parts re-manufactured (those no longer available from the manufacturer). If there's enough demand, someone will find a way to make the part required.

Numerous specialist websites also sell parts for classic bikes, and many BSA and Triumph models have almost complete parts back up available.

MAGAZINES

Magazines should not be overlooked. At the time of writing, there were at least eight classic bike monthly magazines on sale in the UK, most of which are sold internationally, as well as two or three dedicated off-road magazines that are available worldwide. They all have a classified advert section at the back, along with lists of classic bike dealers with parts

2.1 Magazines feature restoration stories, technical articles, and the venues and dates for upcoming auto jumbles, classic dirt bike shows and race/trials meetings.

for sale. This remains a good source of parts, and buying specialist magazines also puts you in touch with experts, such as engine rebuilders, chrome platters, sprayers, powder coating companies, and the like.

SHOWS

During the year, there are a large number of classic motorcycle shows. These shows are well attended, and tend to have a very good variety of motorcycles on display. There is always a good showing of classic off-road models for sale, both whole bikes and parts.

I have found these shows a great way of finding out about newer parts and recent upgrades for bikes. For example, the Yamaha TY trials models: at the time of writing, you can now buy a complete up-rated frame kit, along with just about every other part that you could possible wish for – not bad for a bike that started production in 1974. The same is true for many other models and manufactures.

2.2 A rare CCM 350 on display at the Sammy Miller stand, at the Telford Classic Dirt Bike Show.

Shows also feature our off-road heroes, who give interviews and recount tales of the sort of riding that inspired us at the time.

THE AUTOJUMBLE

The autojumble, or swap meet, is my favourite way of sourcing parts. Imagine, a market full of stalls selling bikes, parts and accessories just for classics, with 1000s of other enthusiasts sorting through boxes looking for the last little part to finish their project.

Although this can be more time-consuming than, say, buying online, at an autojumble you can see the parts close up, haggle with the seller, and take the part away with you that day. Often the seller will be able to advise you on other parts that you may need, or that they may have at home that are also for sale.

There'll be whole bikes for sale, too. Some might look like they've just been dragged out of the local river, but others will be in immaculate condition. Many dealers focus on a particular manufacturer or model, while others have a mix-and-match approach. Lots of the stall holders are traders who sell parts and bikes for a living, whereas others have smaller stalls and may be just selling off parts that they have accumulated from old projects over the years. Either way, in my opinion, this is the most enjoyable way to source parts.

I arrange to meet with my friends, I look out for the parts that they are after, and they look out for mine. Refreshments are always available, and you can have a good day out enjoying your hobby. At the end of the day, I load the car with all the goodies I have bought, feeling satisfied that I have some extra parts to go towards finishing my latest project. I'm not always lucky in finding what I need, but it's always an enjoyable day – and believe me, you never take enough money. Every stall seems to have something you would like to buy, and there is always that other potential project to be seen.

Many sellers at autojumbles have traded like this for years and are knowledgeable and reasonable with their prices.

It's not only used and old parts for sale, you'll find stalls selling new fuel pipes, nuts and bolts, badges, stickers, etc.

Some autojumbles are simply auto markets with parts and bikes for sale, but others are part of a much bigger classic bike show, such as the Stafford Show Ground and Newark.

I am sure you'll find what you need using these sources, and have your project finished in no time.

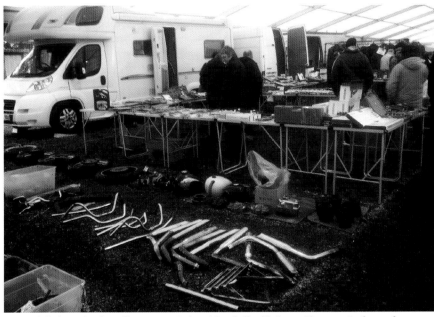

2.3 A typical stall at an autojumble, full of interesting parts for sale.

2.4 A nicely restored Dot trials bike at an autojumble, waiting for a potential buyer.

2.5 11,000 people arrived on a freezing January weekend at a classic bike show in Newark, England, hoping to find the parts they needed.

Chapter 3
Getting started

Begin the initial strip down by assessing the condition of the engine, especially if you haven't heard it run before. Providing that you can get it running at this stage and all seems okay, it will simply be a case of cleaning, polishing or painting it before inserting it back in its frame.

Very important: Before you do anything with the engine, check the oil level and top it up if necessary. Don't get caught out trying to start the engine, only to discover the oil leaked out years ago. Damage caused to the engine when run with no oil will undoubtedly lead to an expensive repair bill, which can be easily avoided.

Start with the basic checks on the ignition and fuel system.

3.1 Off-road bikes have little in the way of electrics, but what there is still needs to be in good condition, so check over now, to save endless hours of investigating possible problems later, or breakdowns while competing.

3.2 Take out the sparkplug and lay it on the cylinder head. Do not hold the sparkplug; hold the plug cap. If you hold the sparkplug, you're likely to get a sharp shock – this is how I found out the electrics were okay on my very first project, to the great amusement of my friends.

Give a good kick on the kickstarter, taking a close look at the sparkplug electrode while you do so. Does it spark? This is what you are looking for. If it sparks, great: the ignition is looking okay. If not, it could be a faulty cap or plug. You can investigate this properly later.

Once you have checked the sparkplug, follow with the checks to the fuel system. For now, you can assume that the fuel tank is clean. Add some fresh fuel and pull the fuel hose from the carburettor, turn on the fuel tap and see if there is fuel coming from it. Only do this briefly (and have a suitable receptacle to catch the fuel), to assess whether you have a clear fuel tap.

Once you know the ignition and fuel systems are okay, you can attempt to start the engine.

Caution! Do this in an open space – not inside a garage or shed – because **exhaust gases are dangerous if inhaled.**

If the engine starts, let it warm up. It may not have been started for years, so do not rev it too much. Listen for strange noises and look for oil leaks.

If there are no obvious problems, you can assume the engine is okay. If, after going through the basic starting check, the engine does not start, you'll need to investigate it later.

Once you've assessed whether the engine is good or not, you can move on to the strip down.

3.3 Checking the fuel tap: have a suitable container handy to catch the fuel.

3.5 The fuel tap has a small filter that easily blocks.

3.4 Turn off the tap. This is a Montesa Cota 349 fuel tap, in the 'off' position.

3.6 Here, the filter is partially blocked by dirt and other debris. Also, we can see that someone has used sealer (indicated by arrow), presumably to prevent or remedy a fuel leak.

STARTING THE STRIP DOWN

It's good practice to make a photographic record of your motorcycle and its parts as it's dismantled. This will provide a record that you can refer back to when reassembling the bike. It is also useful evidence of work done to show to a potential buyer if you ever come to sell the bike.

Tip: When dismantling the bike, it's good practice to put the screws and bolts back in the hole they came from. This both keeps them safe, and means you know their correct location. You can always replace with a newer one later, and you will know the size and type of screw/bolt to use. Also try to group nuts and bolts: for instance, keep all the engine mounting bolts, washers and nuts together in a small box, and label it.

You'll find an impact driver very useful here, particularly on engine casing screws. Make sure you use the correct size spanner, socket or screwdriver the first time you attempt to undo something – all too often people try to undo a screw or nut with the incorrect size tool and this results in a screw or nut that becomes rounded and even more difficult to release. Bolt extractors can help if this happens, but it's far better to remove the item correctly to start with. Some will be very stubborn, and may require a firm clout with the impact wrench, or warming with a blow lamp.

With some nuts, such as those on engine mounting bolts, use a good socket and hold the other end of the bolt firmly with a suitable size spanner to prevent it from turning. Normally, once the nut begins to move, it becomes looser and looser until it come off. If it remains very tight, spray on more light oil as more thread is exposed. This will also help when it comes to the rebuild.

Remove the larger components first, such as the seat and tank, to give you access to other parts.

3.7 Start by spraying nuts, bolts and screws with a light oil, such as GT85, to free any part that is stuck.

3.8 When using an impact wrench, hold it firmly on the nut or in the screw, so that it does not bounce out when hit. Use a club hammer; this will help provide the turning action required alongside the impact, to crack the seal of the seized bolt or nut. Often it's not the thread that is stuck, but the head of the nut or screw. On casing screws, I sometimes give them a light sideways tap to help break the seal against the casing – always being careful not to damage the casing.

3.9 Organize the bolts and screws into containers, and keep them in groups – I place all the engine mounting bolts in one container, so that they do not become mixed with other bolts. Label the containers.

Remove the seat and tank

3.10 This model has an all-in-one seat tank unit, secured front and back with nuts and bolts.

3.11 Remove nuts and bolts from the front and rear of the seat/tank unit.

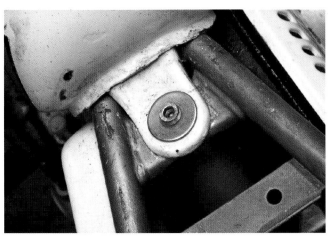

3.12 Many models have the tank secured by a nut and bolt at the rear ...

3.13 ... and the front of the fuel tank held by two brackets that locate onto its rubbers on the frame.

3.14 The fuel tank rubbers on this road bike are very similar to those on Japanese off-roaders.

3.15 Pull the tank backwards and up a little to free it from the location rubbers that are hidden under the front of the fuel tank, if your model has them. Alternatively, simply lift off the tank.

3.16 Once the seat and tank are removed, you can see the condition of the wiring, rubbers and other parts that were covered.

Remove the HT coil and the cables

The cables may be serviceable and, if they look okay, it's worth oiling them with some light oil, as this will help you later.

3.17 Do not pull the wires, as they may come loose in the connector; pull the connector instead.

3.18 Remove the HT coil.

3.19 Pull back dust covers to reveal the cable adjuster.

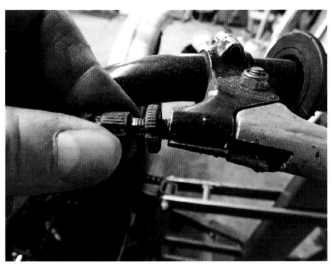

3.20 Loosen the cable adjuster, and line up the slots, so that the cable can be pulled free.

3.21 Pull the nipple from the lever, and remove the cable.

3.22 Now loosen the other end of the cable, and pull free.

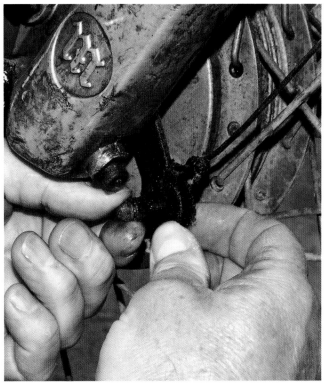

3.23 Follow this procedure with the front brake cable, too.

REMOVING THE ENGINE
The following procedure describes the basics of removing the engine. You will find more detailed instructions in your model-specific workshop manual. Unless you have an engine lift, you will need someone else to assist you.

3.24 Undo the two exhaust manifold fixings. There will either be two exhaust studs or two bolts; perhaps even a screw-on sleeve. Spray with plenty of light oil, because this area is prone to rust, so a dousing of penetrating oil will make removal easier.

3.25 Loosen exhaust clamp nuts (or bolts) ...

3.26 ... and remove the silencer support bolt, too.

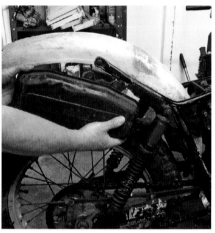

3.27 Remove the exhaust silencer. There is likely to be carbon build-up on the inside of the exhaust, so a twisting action will help separate the two halves.

3.28 On this silencer, there should be two O-ring seals, but these are missing, and will need to be replaced when rebuilding.

3.29 Finally, remove the exhaust pipe.

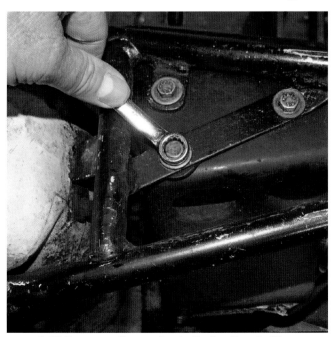

3.30 Remove all securing bolts for the air filter.

3.31 Loosen the jubilee clip that holds the air filter rubber to the carburettor.

3.32 Now remove the complete air filter housing.

3.34 Unscrew the top of the carburettor and pull out the carburettor slide.

3.33 Loosen the jubilee clip that holds the carburettor to the inlet manifold.

3.35 Now remove the carburettor.

Start by removing the exhaust system

At this stage we need to remove the carburettor slide from the cable and refit it to the carburettor, so that the carburettor is in one piece. To do this:

3.36 Push the cable through the bottom of the carburettor slide until you can see the nipple. Then move the cable to the side, so that it can be withdrawn.

3.37 Replace the slide, spring and top cover.

3.38 Now you have a complete carburettor, ready for servicing later.

3.39 Remove the mudguard (fender) rear mounting bolts ...

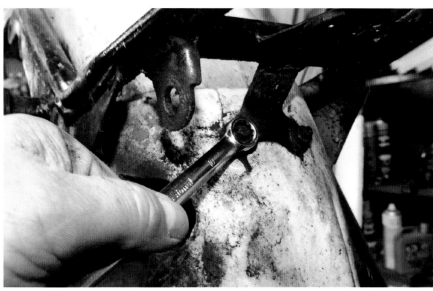

3.40 ... followed by the front mounting bolts.

3.41 Now remove the rear mudguard.

3.42 Locate the split link of the drive chain and remove it. With a pair of pliers, squeezing hard the split link should allow it to pop off of the chain link. If this proves difficult, prise it off with a screwdriver. Degrease it first. This is one of the more dirty jobs on your rebuild.

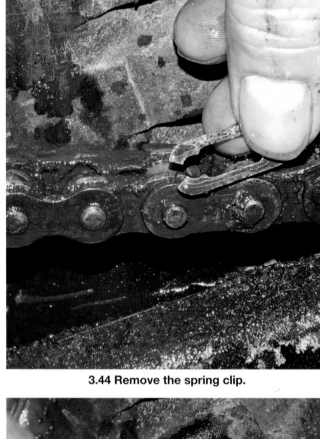

3.44 Remove the spring clip.

3.43 Push forward, from the open end of the spring clip, with a screwdriver or similar tool.

3.45 Remove the side of the link.

3.46 Now you can separate the link fully and remove the chain.

3.48 Remove the rear wheel spindle nut. Carefully note the order of washers, adjusters and spacers, for reassembly.

3.47 Unscrew the torque arm bolts, ready for rear wheel removal.

3.49 Pull the spindle from the rear wheel.

3.50 Once you have removed the spindle, reassemble in reverse order, remembering the position of washers, adjusters and spacers.

Engine removal

3.51 Start to remove all engine mounting bolts.

3.52 There are engine mounting bolts at the rear, the front, and on top of this engine.

3.53 There is also a hidden engine mounting bolt that screws into the engine casing.

Once all bolts are removed, support the engine with a suitable jack and a piece of wood, before removing the engine mounting bolts.

Important: The engine is very heavy, so a suitable engine lift is needed. In the absence of such, ask for assistance when lifting it out of the frame. Never attempt it on your own!

3.54 Once the engine mounting bolts have been removed, the engine can be lifted and placed on a strong bench for inspection later.

3.55 With the engine removed, you can now begin the messy job of cleaning and degreasing the frame.

Years worth of dirt, built up on the sumpguard, should be removed now.

3.56 Scrape off all solid dirt with an old screwdriver or something similar.

3.57 Remove the two rear shock absorbers by unscrewing the top bolts.

3.58 Remove the bottom bolts.

3.59 Loosen top and bottom fork yolk bolts.

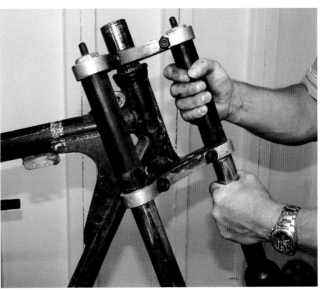

3.60 Once the yoke bolts are loose, pull out the fork legs.

3.61 Next, use a large spanner or socket to unscrew the steering head nut.

3.63 Below the top yoke is the steering bearing nut. Loosen this.

3.62 Then lift off the top yolk.

3.64 Fully unscrew the steering head bolt ...

3.67 When the stem is out, you will be able to remove the remaining bearings.

3.65 … then lift off the steering bearing cover.

3.68 Check inside the top of the steering bearing housing, to see if all the bearings are present, as here.

3.66 Pull out the steering stem, being very careful not to lose any bearings. The bearings will be covered in grease, but it's common for them to fall out; make sure none are lost.

3.69 Remove all the bearings to a safe place for cleaning.

3.70 Unscrew the nuts from the swinging arm spindle.

3.71 Using an old long bolt, gently knock out the spindle.

3.73 With everything now removed from the frame, now look for cracked welds and/or other damage.

Set the swinging arm and frame to one side, for powdercoating or spraying. Be sure to remove the old swinging arm bushes before spraying. If you have other metal items, these can be done at the same time.

If you have decided to have your frame powdercoated, now is the time to send off these parts.

3.72 Once the spindle is removed, you can pull free the whole swinging arm assembly.

3.74 For best results, pressure wash the frame to remove all dirt and grime.

If you're going to spray the larger items, prepare them now. Start by applying degreaser and a small brush, carefully checking for cracks in the frame. Any that you find will need welding/braising.

Once everything is degreased, flatten off old scratches or chip marks.

Apply tape to protect areas you do not want painted. Insert screws in threads to prevent paint getting in.

3.75 You will need a selection of different grades of wet and dry abrasive paper.

3.77 Go over again with a finer grade, such as 240. Make sure the frame is supported well, it will be heavy.

3.76 Start with around 120 grade coarse paper to remove the worst of the rust.

3.78 A multi-tool will save you time and is great for sanding those awkward areas. Remove all old stickers at this stage.

Caution! When spraying, be sure to wear appropriate protective mask and clothing, as the fumes are toxic.

The frame is now finished and ready to be rebuilt.

3.79 A good capacity compressor and spray gun setup are best if you intend to do the spraying yourself.

3.81 Hanging a smaller part makes it easier to spray all sides without touching or moving it.

3.80 If you do not have spraying equipment, good results can be achieved with spray cans. In the case of Hammerite, no priming is necessary and only two coats of the finish gloss are required. I have found these new paints to be very hardwearing, and, for parts such as a swinging arm or stand, a very economical way to achieve a good finish.

3.82 After the first coat of primer, it's likely you'll see one or two areas that need more rubbing down. Until the first coat goes on, not all faults can be seen properly. Now spray the whole frame with two coats of primer. Patience is the key with spraying, so make sure each coat is 100 per cent dry, before applying the finishing coats.

3.83 Apply two coats of the finish gloss. Go over the whole frame (or the most visible areas, if you want to save some time) with a very fine wet and dry paper such as 800-1000 grade. By doing this, you'll get a much shinier gloss finish.

3.84 Spray all black items at the same time. These will include the swinging arm and stands, but can also include engine mounting brackets.

Chapter 4
Cleaning & polishing

Now that you have a newly painted or powdercoated frame, it's time to turn your attention to the other parts of the motorcycle. Each item must be cleaned and polished to bring it to the best possible finish. Parts may be too rusty or damaged to salvage, or may need sending off for chrome plating.

Start by thoroughly cleaning each part, so you can assess its condition, and guarantee the good working order of all components.

SAFETY TIPS BEFORE YOU START

- Always use safety equipment – dust mask, safety goggles and gloves
- Always apply the item being finished to the area of the polishing mop which is rotating away from you
- Cover and tie up long hair to prevent entanglement with machines
- Fasten loose cuffs and loose clothing. Remove or secure long necklaces to prevent entanglement
- If the polishing wheel 'grabs' the item being polished, let it go, do not hold on

DEGREASING

Engine and frame parts will need to be degreased. Smaller parts can be placed in a bucket and cleaned with a suitable degreasing agent and a small paint brush, while larger parts, such as the frame, need to be cleaned in an area that will suffer least from the mess that can result. Standing a frame on end against a wall in a large plastic container, such as an old baby bath, works well and keeps the dirt contained.

The degreaser must be rinsed off and the parts dried as soon as possible. This is particularly important with ferrous parts that will quickly rust again, if not dried and protected appropriately.

ULTRASONIC CLEANING

Ultrasonic cleaners use ultrasound vibrations and an appropriate cleaning solvent (sometimes just ordinary tap water) to clean small or delicate items. Many larger cleaners have a temperature control right up

4.1 A free-standing parts washer can be very useful.

4.2 Smaller items, such as carburettors, can be thoroughly cleaned in an ultrasonic cleaner. Available in a variety of sizes, smaller cleaners are suitable for very small parts, such as carburettor jets. Larger cleaners can accommodate a whole carburettor. This is by far the best way to clean carburettors.

to 80°C. The combination of ultrasonic vibrations of around 23,000kHz and heat make a very good cleaning agent. Originally used to sterilise surgical instruments, these machines are now available to buy at reasonable prices. Sizes refer the amount of liquid they can hold, and the dimensions of the basket the parts are held in.

4.3 A carburettor before ultrasonic cleaning ...

4.4 ... the same carburettor a few minutes later. Not only is the outside clean, but, more importantly, the tiny passageways inside the carburettor body are dirt-free.

EQUIPMENT

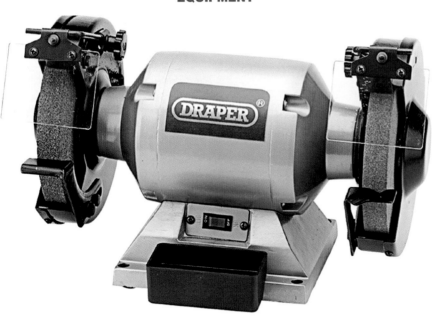

4.5 Polishing wheels have been adapted to fit a wide range of garage equipment, the most common of which is the bench grinder.

4.7 One of the grinding wheels is removed and replaced by the polishing mop mandrel. The mandrel is simply a spiral attachment that allows quick and easy fitting and removal of polishing mop heads. You can also purchase dedicated polishing machines.

4.8 The polishing mop is screwed onto the mandrill, and the rotation of the spindle keeps it secure.

4.6 With the grinder bolted to the bench, you can apply the required pressure to the part being polished.

4.9 Attachments are also available for pillar and hand drills.

WHEELS – METAL POLISHING & COMPOUNDS

Alloy responds well to polishing and, with the correct equipment, anyone can achieve great results.

Alloy parts, such as fork legs, engine casing and control levers, can be polished to a high standard. Polishing kits are great value for money, and come with a selection of polishing wheels and compound bars of different grade polishing wax. The wax slowly melts away, leaving the abrasive to polish/cut the metal. If too much wax is used a residue will be left on the metal surface. This can be removed with white spirit and a clean cloth.

Polishing is much the same as sanding, using progressively finer and finer abrasives, each one cutting out the marks left by the previous one. The combination of different grade polishing waxes and polishing mop wheels will leave a high shine finish when the process is completed.

POLISHING MOPS

There are three grades of polishing mops:

Sisal metal polishing mops
These are very fast cutting and hard, they are used for first stage polishing operations with Brown metal polishing compound on soft metals including aluminium, brass and copper and Black metal polishing compound on hard metals including steel and stainless steel.

Colour stitch metal polishing mops
These are versatile cutting mops used for general metal polishing which can be used for first stage polishing with Brown metal polishing compound on soft metals including aluminium, brass and copper or for second stage polishing on hard metals with the Green, Pink and White metal polishing compounds.

Loose fold metal polishing mops
Most popular of the three, these mops can be used with the Blue, Green, Pink, White and Rouge metal polishing compounds. Loose fold metal polishing mops are 100 per cent white soft cotton, with no

hard pieces. The mops have centre washers, no staples, and have been finished so they can be used straight away.

Polishing compounds
- Brown – For first cut and flattening on non-ferrous metals
- Blue – For final finishing on non-ferrous metals
- Black – For first cut and flattening on steels
- Green – For final finishing on steels
- Pink – For final high polish finishing on chrome and steels
- White – For final high polish finishing on stainless steels
- Rouge – For polishing soft precious metals such as gold and silver
- Vienna Lime (White Powder) – For removing polishing compound and grease residues

The polishing kits will not remove metal, and if parts are heavily scratched, marked or scored,

4.10 If the alloy has deep scratches, these must be removed before you can start polishing. Use a fine metal file, and file lightly in different directions until the scratch or dent has gone.

4.11 Once the scratch is filed out, use wet and dry paper of around 400 grade to sand the filed areas, ensuring that you dip it regularly in clean water and soap solution. This removes the alloy particles and keeps the paper clean and effective.

then suitable abrasives should be used to remove scratches, such as fine file, wet and dry paper, rubbing blocks.

Once the marks left by the file have been sanded down, use 600 grade to continue sanding down until marks left by the 400 grade paper have been removed. Continue, until you get a completely smooth surface ready to be polished. Clean and degrease the part (using the appropriate degreaser) before you polish.

Polishing

Begin with the coarser, harder polishing wheel know as Sisal.

Once the drill or polisher is rotating, lightly touch the mop head with the grey wax bar, apply sparingly for two seconds. The dark grey bar is a coarser compound than the white bar and should be used first.

When all scratches/marks are removed, and the part has a uniform matt finish, remove the sisal metal polishing mop. It's very important that you remove all marks/scratches and

leave a uniform finish for each grade of wax used.

Re-polish with the softer wheel, as before, going over the whole area. Patience is the key here. If you require a highly polished finish, you will need to keep going over the piece with finer polishing bars until you reach the shine you're want. Using a clean cloth, go over the polished article with the white Vienna Lime Powder to remove grease left on the surface. Buff with a clean cotton cloth to finish.

4.12 Offer the piece to be polished to the wheel, applying medium to hard pressure. Go over the whole surface several times, until the worst oxidisation has been removed. Always vary the direction of the polishing mop over the surface you're polishing, even if only by a few degrees – how much you can do so will depend the item's shape. If you come across scratches, polish across, rather than along, them.

4.13 This is the finished fork leg, looking as good as new. Polishing can be taken further if you require a mirror-type finish.

On larger parts, use the polishing wheels as you did with the alloy parts, but use the soft wheel and fine wax right away. Wet and dry paper or the coarser wax are too harsh for chrome.

RUST REMOVAL
Parts will inevitably have rusted to some degree. Some may be completely corroded and no longer of use, whereas others may not be in such bad condition.

There are products on the market that will remove light surface rust and can also, sometimes, help to loosen rusted parts, or even completely remove some quite bad rust.

On lightly rusted parts, you can use any mild acid, such as vinegar, lemon juice, or even cola. Soaking the required parts overnight is the easiest option – allow plenty of time to soak to get good results.

On larger and more awkward parts, use a large bowl. An old plastic baby bath is perfect, and normally large enough to hold most motorcycle parts. Parts will need to be degreased first, with a degreaser and small

Use smaller mops for difficult to reach areas.

Chrome polishing
Chrome-plated parts are always the focus of attention on motorcycles, and it's always satisfying when your hard work begins to shine, literally. On smaller parts, use a cream paste, such as Autosol, with a clean cloth to clean and remove light rust.

4.14 Light rust on this wheel rim can easily be removed with a suitable chrome polish.

4.15 Here is a good example of some serious polishing on a classic motorcycle – hard to believe that, at the time of writing, this bike is almost 60 years old!

brush; rinsed away as instructed by the manufacturer.

Lots of rust removers are concentrated, and can be diluted to make around 20 litres of solution. Most need to be at room temperature to work effectively, and parts are normally left overnight to soak. Follow the instructions supplied. Once everything is cleaned, you can decide if parts need to be sent off for re-plating.

4.16 After the rust is removed, many parts, such as these Suzuki 'S' bolts, can be buffed on the polishing wheel and re-used.

After using rust remover, rinse the cleaned part and give it a light spray with light oil, such as GT-85 to prevent rust from returning.

For more heavy-duty rust or paint removal, you could use a shot-blasting cabinet, such as the one in photo 4.18. This works on compressed air from a compressor, and blasts different grades of media at high pressure onto the piece being cleaned. The rust is removed, leaving bare metal.

These are also used on engine crank cases, heads and barrels.

Before I purchased my first blast cabinet, I enquired about having some parts cleaned. The price quoted for blasting two parts was over half the cost of buying the blasting cabinet, so the blast cabinet soon paid for itself. Although the blast cabinet is an effective tool for cleaning heavily soiled and rusted parts, proceed with caution with soft alloys and other delicate surfaces. These cabinets are powerful, and

4.17 The footrest on the right spent ten minutes in rust remover. This needed to be dried quickly, to prevent rust forming again.

4.18 A small cabinet blaster is an asset to your workshop. These connect to a compressor and have a blast gun inside the cabinet. Different grades of media can be added to the cabinet to blast off rust and dirt. The blast media is recycled inside the cabinet, and can be used several times. It's a dry process, and items to be blasted should first be free from grease.

4.19 The cylinder head will require a de-coke before the rebuild.

4.20 This is the same cylinder head after a few minutes in the blasting cabinet, with all carbon deposits now removed. It's a quick, clean process, and recommended for cleaning a variety of motorcycle parts.

you will need to use the correct blast media according to the surface being blasted. For a motorcycle sidestand that is made of steel, you could use a coarse media such as iron, whilst for a cylinder barrel, as in the pictures above, you would use much softer crushed walnut shells.

DIY CHROME PLATING

Classic motorcycles have a large proportion of visible metal chrome-plated. This gives a pleasing appearance and protects the base metal underneath. A finished bike, when polished, is the pride and joy of its owner, who can spend hours polishing it. Unfortunately, over the years, road grime and salt takes its toll on chrome-plating, resulting in rusty, pitted chrome areas.

You have several options. You can polish these areas with some off-the-shelf chrome polish, or replace it with a good condition secondhand part.

You can send the part off to be re-chromed. There are numerous companies that offer this service and the results can be very good, with a finished article looking like new. It's by far the best option, but not the cheapest.

You could also try DIY chrome-plating. Kits have become more readily available over the last few years, and can give (with a little patience and practice) some acceptable results. Most DIY kits are more suited to the smaller parts of the bike, such as brackets, nuts, bolts and spindles. The dome bolts that hold down the handlebar clamps, the heads of the nuts and bolts that hold the front and rear mudguards (fenders) are in full view, and always in chrome. These bolts could be replaced – however, lots of manufacturers have their logo stamped on bolts: Suzuki places its small 'S' logo on many of its bolts; and stamped or unusual bolts will be difficult to source. Restoring them might be a better option.

Replica chrome-plating kits give a good enough finish to satisfy the average restorer. They are relatively inexpensive, quite easy to use, and run off a small car battery charger. They do not take up much room, and, in the long run, they'll save money.

There are some chemicals involved, but all kits come with instruction and safety advice. If you buy a kit, always follow the manufacturer's instructions. These can often be found on the manufacturer's website and it's worth reading these beforehand, to help you decide if this option is suitable for you.

The Replica basic kit consists of:

- Chrome electrolyte chemicals (will make five litres)
- Chrome brightener
- Chrome maintenance
- Chrome anodes
- A thermostatic tank heater
- A tank
- Titanium wire
- Copper wire
- Brown wire
- Blue wire
- A variable current controller which enables you to use a 6-12v car battery or charger to plate items of different sizes
- Crocodile clips
- Goggles
- A dust mask
- Gloves
- A chrome electroplating guide
- Safety data sheets

VISIT VELOCE ON THE WEB – WWW.VELOCE.CO.UK
All current books • New book news • Special offers • Gift vouchers • Forum

46

Chapter 5
Engine

A wonderful array of motorcycle engines are used in off-road competition. Those used in scrambling (or motocross as it's now known) are tuned for maximum power, while, in trials competition,

5.1 At one time, this would have been an ideal candidate for off-road conversion.

47

5.3 … by comparison, this small two-stroke James is light and nimble, and was competing at the same event.

5.2 A wonderful old BSA with a single cylinder four-stroke engine, giving plenty of low-down grunt – just what is needed for trials riding. These engines are relatively heavy compared to a two-stroke, but are sought-after in Pre '65 trials …

torque is more desirable. Generally speaking, these engines are one- or two-cylinder, and can be split into two-stroke and four-stroke.

In the early days of motorcycle competition, the bikes and engines were almost the same as the road-going version. Often, manufacturers never made a competition model; competitors themselves upgraded their road bikes for trials or scrambles.

ENGINE UNIT

This chapter is not a rebuild guide for every model. Instead, it uses the example of a Montesa 349 two-stroke trials engine to help give you an idea of what you're likely to come across when stripping and rebuilding the engine, and what to look out for.

There are plenty of comprehensive motorcycle manuals that give very good step-by-step guides to stripping and rebuilding a particular engine, and, with the correct tools and guidance, many tasks are not too difficult for the first time restorer.

Some work may need to be carried out by a motorcycle engineering workshop, due to the precision or equipment required. However, you can save a huge amount of money if you do as much of the rebuild as you can – or, at least, carry out some repairs to the engine yourself. The feeling you get when you first start an engine that you have built yourself is great. Better still, if you *have* gone to the trouble of carrying out your own rebuild, and something goes wrong at a later date, you will have the know how to

5.4 CZ was very successful in scrambling, winning seven world motocross championships in the 1960s, and was the first to use expansion chambers in the exhaust system. It also won many International Six-Day Trials from the 1940s right up to1980s.

5.5 We will be stripping a **Montesa 349** two-stroke trials engine in this chapter.

5.7 Damaged threads and heads: it's likely that you will come across some damaged threads, bolt or screw heads. Female threads are repairable using a Helicoil kit, which comes with all parts necessary. The main one to look for is the Sparkplug thread. If this is very badly damaged, it could be a machine shop fix and a little expensive; however, it is a repairable problem.

5.8 Kickstart and gearbox shafts: check that these have good splines. They will often be worn which will require a replacement, because it's not easy to repair properly, or access while the shaft is still inside the engine.

solve the problem much more quickly yourself.

With the engine safely on the bench, cleaned with suitable degreaser, start your inspection. Have a good look at it: do you notice cracks or leaks? Screws or bolts with damaged threads? There are almost always some, and you will have to get them out before you can proceed with an internal inspection.

What you will need

There are certain parts that it's advisable to change on your restoration project, some service parts, others mechanical.

- A gasket set. Always buy a full engine gasket set, even if you do not always strip the whole engine. The spare gaskets and seals will come in useful later, and buying the full gasket set is more cost-effective than buying individual gaskets. Some seals are not included in every set, so check what's missing, and try to get hold of these separately, if needed
- Remember that you will also need fresh oil when you re-build the engine. Buy the oil recommended by the manufacturer. Don't forget a new oil filter if your bike uses one
- Sparkplugs and air filter

- Clutch plates. These do wear during normal use. Clutch plates are not expensive, are easy to source, and not difficult to replace

These items are common to many engine types. Refer to the user manual for your specific motorbike when carrying out the following tasks.

What to look for on an external inspection

This can be done with the engine still in the frame.

5.6 Generally, fin damage is only a cosmetic issue, and does not affect the engine's performance, unless the fins are severely damaged, which could lead to overheating problems. Damaged fins will certainly affect the future resale value of your motorcycle.

5.9 Damaged casings or crankcase. Check for cracks and oil leaks, particularly on motorcycles that may have been used off-road and had a harder life than the average motorcycle. Cracks can be repaired if not too large; however, *this* is not how a repair should look.

What to look for on a semi-internal inspection

First, make sure you drain the oil into a suitable container, before detaching the side covers on the engine. Next, remove the side casings, to assess parts of the engine such as the clutch and starter mechanism.

Removing either of the side casings will allow access to the end of the crankshaft. This is most likely to be the generator cover or

5.10 Drain oil, before removing the side casings.

5.13 Once the side casings are off, remove all old gaskets or sealant. You'll quite often find that the engine has had some relatively recent work carried out, and sealant is still present.

5.11 With this casing removed, you can see the magneto, which, on this Montesa trials engine, is typically heavy, helping to give more torque.

5.14 First impressions are good here, with no obviously broken parts inside, and no iron filings in the oil, either. Unusually, the clutch plates of this Montesa engine are held in the clutch basket by metal pins that are only removable by using a press, which compresses the basket in order to release them. I will therefore also show a clutch that has a more conventional system of holding in the plates: namely, bolts or screws (see photos 5.19 and 5.21).

5.12 Next, remove the other casing, to reveal the clutch.

the ignition cover. Either will allow you to feel for end play (slack) in the crankshaft. There should be no sideways movement; if there is, it indicates worn bearings and must be corrected. It's recommended that this is carried out by a professional (see end of this chapter).

5.15 After removing the clutch basket on a previous restoration, the clutch plates were found in pieces. Some smaller parts were found in the bottom of the clutch housing, too.

The colour of the oil will give a good indication of the engine's internal condition. The oil should look similar to runny honey, and be clear, not milky-white or black. It should be smooth to the touch; not gritty.

5.16 Check the condition of the oil. Water has got into the casing of this engine, turning the oil milky. It's most likely to be the result of a faulty seal. The cause must be found and rectified before the engine is reassembled.

5.17 This engine has a secondary flywheel, to help slow engine running. There is locking wire, here, that will need to be cut, before the large nut can be unscrewed.

5.18 Once the clutch cover is off, all parts should look reasonably clean, as seen above. They should have a visible film of oil, with all mechanical parts looking sound. Look for broken metal pieces in the bottom of casings, and visible damage. All nuts and bolts on the inside of an engine should be in very good condition; damaged pieces should be renewed. If the clutch plates are worn or damaged, replace them, too.

5.19 Replacing clutch plates is a very easy task, and, with a new set being relatively inexpensive, I would recommend always replacing old with new.

5.20 The clutch plates are held in by six bolts for this basket – the most common type, and much the easiest to renovate. Loosen each bolt a little at a time, and evenly.

TWO-STROKE ENGINES

The two-stroke, or two-cycle, engine is a simpler design than the four-stroke. It does not have cylinder head valves, cams, camchains, tappets or pushrods, so there is no valve adjustment or valve timing to carry out.

Two-stroke engines rev much higher than the early four-stroke engines, and, being lighter, they have a better power-to-weight ratio. This is particularly useful on a scamble/motocross racer, but can also be tuned for low engine speeds and more torque when required as on a trials machine. The power delivery of a two-stoke engine is normally more peaky than that of a four-stroke that usually has a lower rev range but more low down engine torque available. Motorcycles with a two-stroke engine are generally considered to be more 'thirsty' (use more fuel) than the four-stroke motorcycles of a similar engine capacity.

5.21 A Yamaha twin cylinder two-stroke engine showing the inlet port, piston and exhaust port, along with the clutch mechanism. This is a road-going model, but demonstrates how the engine works without the use of valves, tappets, etc, that are found on a four-stroke engine.

5.22 You can get a good indication of the cylinder condition by carrying out a compression test before dismantling the bike. This applies to four-strokes as well as two-strokes. A low compression level in a cylinder indicates a leak in the engine, most likely through worn piston rings or a damaged head or base gasket. Therefore, more investigation is needed. Correct compression levels for the engine can be found in the relevant workshop manual.

All two-stroke engines use a mixture of two-stroke oil and petrol. The oil keeps the engine lubricated. On older motorcycles, the two-stroke oil and petrol were pre-mixed manually, and then poured into the fuel tank. Later, manufacturers designed bikes with a separate oil tank, and an oil pump that mixed the two-stroke oil automatically as the bike was ridden. Yamaha's was called Autolube, and Suzuki's CCI. The automatic system used less oil, and was more convenient for the rider. There was even an oil reservoir-viewing window or a low oil warning light; sometimes both. However, to save weight, riders often removed the automatic system, and reverted to pre-mixing.

Generally, there is less maintenance to carry out on a two-stroke engine than a four-stroke. The biggest disadvantages of two-strokes is that they burn oil; and use more fuel than a four-stroke of similar size, because they are high revving.

A compression test will give you a good indication of the condition of the cylinder (see photo 5.22). If the compression is too low, you will need to remove the cylinder head to make a more thorough inspection.

The cylinder head on a two-stroke can be unbolted and taken

5.24 Once the bolts are removed, the head simply pulls off. If you find it a little stuck, resist the temptation to lever it off with a screwdriver, or clout it with a hammer. The best and safest way I have found is to gently tap around the edges with a rubber mallet. This normally frees the head without damaging the fins, etc.

off in a few minutes, and then bolted back on with a new gasket. This will give you a good idea of the condition of the engine – you'll see the cylinder bores and the piston crown, as well as the underside of the cylinder head itself. Note that the head bolts should be unbolted in a set pattern, shown in the workshop manual. The bolts are tightened in the same pattern, and also tightened a specific amount. This is called the torque. You will need a torque wrench to do this. The torque settings will be listed in the workshop manual.

Now is a good opportunity to de-coke the cylinder head – removing all old carbon deposits back to the metal. Try not to scratch the head while removing the carbon.

5.23 Removing the cylinder head is a simple task on a two-stroke engine: just remove the head bolts (they must be unbolted in a set order. See workshop manual). Note how thin this head is compared to a four-stroke, because there is no valve mechanism on a two-stroke.

5.25 A two-stroke head from the Montesa 349 before de-coking.

Try not to let anything drop into the cylinder bores. Pad the bore with some clean cloth to block it while you're inspecting. If something drops into the cylinder, it will most likely find its way into the engine crankcase – this will mean a major engine strip down.

Check to see if the bores are scratched or scored. Check the gap between the piston and the cylinder. The tolerances will be in the workshop manual. The piston crown should be tan in colour. This gives an indication of how rich or lean the engine was running. Too dark, and the engine is running too rich; too light, and it's running too lean. The latter can cause a two-stroke engine to seize, so it really is important to check this and set the fuel mixture correctly.

If a cylinder bore is not in an acceptable condition, you will need to remove the cylinder. In order to

5.26 The head off showing the cylinder bore. You can just see the top of the transfer ports. This cylinder is showing little sign of wear.

do so, you will need to remove the carburettors and exhaust system first.

Once those are out of the way, slowly pull the barrels up. Sometimes they come easily; sometimes they take some persuading. If the head is stuck, give it a gentle tap all around with a rubber mallet. Usually this does the trick. Try to tap somewhere firm, not on any of the cooling fins, if you can help it.

Once you have broken the seal and the cylinder starts to rise, do not let anything drop into the crankcase. Use more clean cloth to block the crankcase, and be careful.

Now continue to lift the barrel. You may have a single barrel, or separate barrels. Remember the pistons will be at different heights if you have a twin cylinder engine. You need to lift the barrel, while, at the same time, holding the connecting

5.27 Before you remove the cylinder fully, make sure you support the piston so that it does not drop down and get damaged.

rod (or conrod as it's commonly known) that is now becoming exposed, to prevent the piston falling and hitting the barrel studs: it would be advisable to have an assistant help with this.

If there are no scores in the cylinder, nor problems with the piston, count yourself lucky: it's unlikely that you will need to carry out a re-bore (if the compression was good, that is).

If you find that you have a scored barrel or cracked piston, you will need to have the cylinder re-bored and a new piston fitted. This should be carried out at a professional engine service workshop. It's usual, when changing the piston, to renew the small end bearing at the same time.

5.31 Clean off old gasket remains.

Do not forget to replace the cylinder base gasket, before putting back the cylinder.

5.28 Once the barrel is fully removed, plug the crankcase with some clean cloth to prevent debris falling in. You can now check the piston rings and properly measure the piston itself. Check for play (movement up and down) in the big and small end bearings: there should be no play in either. If there is, you will need to renew the relevant components.

5.29 You may find that the piston rings are worn and need replacing. Note the small peg, and shape of the ring ends that go under it. This ensures the rings are the correct way round.

5.30 The crown of a piston clearly showing the arrow to help ensure the piston is facing in the right direction. This piston needs to be de-coked.

5.32 Carefully lift out the spring clip. Wear safety glasses when doing this, as it can spring out at speed, and hit you in the eye.

5.33 Find a socket of a similar size to the gudgeon pin and slowly push out the pin.

5.35 Next, remove the small end roller bearing.

5.34 Once the gudgeon pin has been pushed out, pull free the piston.

5.36 Always use a new complete gasket set when rebuilding the engine.

5.37 When replacing the small end bearing, add a little two-stroke oil. This ensures the bearing isn't dry on initial start-up once it has been rebuilt.

5.38 Refit the piston, ensuring that nothing drops into the crankcase.

5.39 Now replace the piston rings, and ensure that they're aligned with the pegs in the ring groove. (Not all pistons have pegs: if that is the case, have the gaps of the piston rings at least 120° away from each other.)

small amount of two-stroke oil, so the piston slips in nicely. The piston should slip in reasonably easily – never force it. If it gets stuck, it's most likely that the barrel is caught on part of the piston ring. Make sure the rings are the right way up, and that the piston and rings are facing in the right direction. Normally, there is a small peg in the piston ring groove: this is where the two ends of the piston ring should be, to help you set the piston ring facing in the correct direction. If the rings are over the pegs, they won't sit back in the groove as they should, and will catch on the piston.

When you come to replace the piston and head, it will help if you have piston ring compressors to hold the rings in place when lowering the barrel. However, you can fit pistons and rings without these if you're careful, by simply squeezing the rings in, and holding them until the cylinder has slipped over them.

Lightly oil the cylinder with a

5.41 Lower the head carefully.

5.40 If your bike has a single cylinder, like the Montesa 349 here, once the barrel is back in place, turn the engine until the piston is at top dead centre. This prevents anything falling into the cylinder when refixing the head. On some models, there are bolts for securing the barrel before refitting the cylinder head, but, on others, the head bolts are the same as those that hold down the barrel. If you have a two-cylinder engine, follow the instructions in the workshop manual.

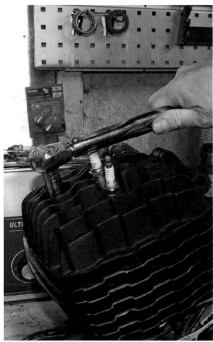

5.42 Use a torque wrench to tighten the cylinder head in accordance with the workshop manual: it will give the correct torque, and the correct tightening sequence.

5.43 Replace the side casings. Use new gaskets, as before.

Once the barrels are back in place, you can replace the head gasket and head. Now tighten the head bolts/nuts down in sequence and to the correct torque, as described in the workshop manual. It is very important that this is done correctly, to make sure the head is not distorted and the gasket sits well.

You have now carried out a top end rebuild on the engine. Bottom end rebuilds are much more involved and, for most first-time restorers, best left to the professionals. I will, however, go through the main procedures later in this chapter.

FOUR-STROKE ENGINES

Many of the procedures in the two-stroke section also apply to this section, so, here, I will go through the main differences when working on a four-stroke or four-cycle engine.

The main difference between a four-stroke and a two-stroke engine is that the four-stroke engine has inlet and exhaust valves, which need a mechanism to drive them. The inlet valve opens to allow the fuel/air mixture from the carburettor into the cylinder. It then closes. Both the inlet and exhaust valves stay closed for the compression stroke. The fuel/air mixture is compressed by the upward movement of the piston and, at the right moment (normally a fraction before the piston reaches top dead centre), a spark is introduced, igniting the fuel and creating combustion.

Once the engine has fired, the piston is forced down and the exhaust valve opens to allow the spent gasses to escape. This happens thousands of times a minute, and has to be timed very precisely. Each valve has to open an exact amount, the tappet that operates the valve is adjusted to a few thousandths of an inch. If the valves are adjusted incorrectly, the valve will either open at the wrong moment, or for the incorrect length of time: in each case, the engine will run badly or not at all.

5.45 Two pistons, both from four-stroke engines: note the third ring, at the bottom, is an oil scraper ring.

5.44 This wonderful Matchless four-stroke engine was widely used in off-road competition. Note the depth of the head, due to the camshaft and valve gear, compared to a two-stroke cylinder head.

5.46 Here is a new 50 oversize piston for a four-stroke engine. Note the cutouts for the valves.

The valves are operated by tappets, in turn operated by a pushrod, gears, or now, more commonly, a camshaft or double camshafts. If they are operated by a camshaft, this will be run by a camchain that has some sort of chain tensioner.

5.47 Four valves from a four-stroke engine. You can also see the valve springs and collets.

After many hours of use, valves need to be re-ground in the valve seats. This is a simple process once they are out.

5.49 Paste is applied to the valve seat.

5.48 Some valve lapping paste and a lapping tool (basically two rubber suction cups on a small wooden handle).

5.50 The valve is positioned into the seat without springs, and the lapping tool pushed onto the head as shown.

5.51 Use a backward and forward twisting motion with the lapping tool. This will grind the valve into the seat, and, when done correctly, will give a gas-tight seal that will help with starting and running the engine.

The grinding paste tin has two ends, with a lid at each end. One end has coarse paste, and the other fine paste. Start with the coarse paste, then follow this with the fine paste.

5.52 When finished, the valve and seat should look polished.

The bottom end of the engine has to be timed precisely with the top end, so that, when the piston is at top dead centre (TDC) on the compression stroke, both valves are completely closed. If either is not, the gasses won't be compressed, and won't fire. In the worst case scenario, the piston could hit a valve, causing major engine damage.

Valves that are old may need to be changed, or at least re-lapped, which involves finely polishing the face of the valve and the valve seat, so the valve sits properly, and gives a gas tight seal.

Certain components of the cylinder head will need to be set precisely for the engine to run correctly. The camshaft needs to be set to match the crankshaft, so that the cams are in the correct position for each valve, relevant to each piston. The tappets need to be adjusted to the correct gap, so that they open for the correct amount of time.

If you want to inspect the piston on a four-stroke, you will need to reset all the above, when you replace the head. Removing the head is more involved than if you were removing that of a two-stroke, because you have the camchain and camshaft to tackle. But, once the camchain is loosened, you can pull the cam out and lift off the head.

The older pushrod-type engine head will come off relatively easy.

If your four-stroke engine has stood around for some time, it is likely that, when it starts for the first time (if this is even possible, before you have restored it), it will smoke. Either the rings will be stuck in, allowing oil past, or the valve stem seals will be ruined. Both of these will need to be rectified. On the whole, it is rare to get away with not rebuilding the cylinder head on a four-stroke. You can attempt this yourself – there are some special tools needed, such as a valve spring compressor – or you may conclude that, like a bottom end build, it would be better to leave this to the experts. If you decide to do it yourself, the workshop manual will have a detailed step-by-step guide.

Inspecting the pistons, rings and ends is the same as it with the two-stroke engine.

THE BOTTOM END

I mentioned before that first-time restorers are more likely to tackle a top end rebuild themselves than a bottom end one – more likely left to the professionals.

Bottom end engine rebuilds are done in the instance of problems with a main bearing or a big end bearing. The main engine crankcases will need to be taken apart to allow access to the crankshaft.

5.53 You may have a damaged piston, and splitting the engine will be necessary to get to the crank cases. Here, you can see parts from a broken piston skirt, which must be removed before successfully rebuilding the engine ...

5.55 The process requires the use of at least a few special tools.

Then there is the crankshaft itself. This could well need new main bearing, or require re-grinding.

Both these procedures are carried out in an engine workshop by a professional.

5.54 ... this is quite complex, involving removing the clutch, the gears, the kickstart mechanism, and other components.

5.56 This crankshaft seal was found to be split, so replacing it was unavoidable. The spring has broken out of its seal.

5.57 The crankshaft's component parts separated.

5.58 A heavy hydraulic press is needed to separate the crankshaft components; this is definitely a job for a professional.

5.59 When the crankshaft is reassembled, alignment must be checked thoroughly using dial gauges.

Once the engine is fully stripped down, you can replace all the seals and gaskets, and inspect parts, such as the gears, clutch, etc, as you go. Check with the workshop manual for all the parts to be replaced. If you aren't so confident with an engine, you may want to let the professionals carry out bottom end work.

VISIT VELOCE ON THE WEB – WWW.VELOCE.CO.UK
All current books • New book news • Special offers • Gift vouchers • Forum

64

Chapter 6
Brakes & wheels

Almost every project I have worked on has had brakes that needed restoring. In the past, I have bought projects that were seemingly almost finished, only to find on closer inspection that the front brake has no brake shoes or a similar fault. Make sure you check these important parts. Many projects advertised are loosely assembled for photo purposes and need thoroughly checking over, so please take a very close look at all the brake system components.

I make it a rule now to refurbish all brake components as a matter of course, on all my projects. Like carburettor rebuilds, it is not often you can get away with it. This is one task always on my list of 'must do' jobs on every restoration project.

All classic off-road motorcycles use drum brakes. Disk brakes came along later and are not covered in this book, simply because they were not available on off-road models of the period.

CABLE OR ROD DRUM BRAKES
Cable- and rod-operated drum brakes are relatively easy to restore, and mostly only need stripping, cleaning and reassembling with new brake shoes. Occasionally, you will find that the actuator arm has seized and will need freeing and re-greasing.

Do check all brake cables for correct routing. A cable may have been added hastily for the purpose of a photo, or to make the bike look more complete. A cable that is not routed correctly could tighten when the handlebars are turned, activating

6.1 If the actuator arm is seized, re-grease it.

the brakes and catching you out when riding. This has happened to me in the past.

Check for frayed cables. If a cable is frayed, it will not return correctly, and could result in sticky brakes, causing them to bind and wear out prematurely.

Oiling cables

This method has been used for years, and is still effective today. It can be used on all cables on the bike.

Find somewhere that you can hang the cables quite high, so they don't touch the floor. Use a piece of plasticine to make a small funnel tight to the cable (see photo 6.2). Hang the cable, making sure to place a suitable container under it, to catch oil. Pour a small amount of light oil into the funnel. After 24 hours, the cable will be fully oiled and ready to fit back onto the bike. If you have a cable that is frayed or damaged, replace it with a new one.

This method will work on all cables, even lightly corroded ones. However, I've had cables that are so corroded, they just snapped under light pressure – if you have any doubt about them, change them. You don't want to be miles from home and have a cable break. At best, it is inconvenient; at worst, it can be very dangerous.

6.2 Use plasticine to make a small funnel tight round the end of the cable (see above).

WHEELS

On classic off-road bikes, wheel rims come in plain steel, chrome-plated, stainless, and alloy; the vast majority, with alloy wheels.

6.3 Akront is a Spanish alloy wheel maker, supplying wheels to many bike manufacturers.

Often wheels are in poor condition: check that the wheels are not buckled or damaged, and that all the spokes are tight. Check alloy wheels for hairline cracks and chips.

If you're lucky, a good clean and polish will bring the wheels up like new. Otherwise, they may need rebuilding.

It can sometimes be cheaper to source a good used wheel, rather than have a wheel completely rebuilt. If the rims are in very bad condition, or are damaged, new ones can be bought. The wheels will need to be stripped down and completely rebuilt. The spokes are taken out and the hubs checked over, before the wheels are re-assembled.

Wheel rebuilding is a specialist job, and I would not advise an amateur to undertake this task. However, there are elements that you can undertake to improve a wheel's overall appearance.

The brake hubs, if not polished, often have a painted centre which can be repainted, making a whole lot of difference to the finished look of the motorcycle.

6.4 Start by removing the spindle and taking off the wheel ...

6.5 ... then remove the brake hubs. They simply pull out.

6.8 Check that the grease nipple isn't seized or blocked.

6.6 The spring may be rusty, but will normally clean-up okay with a small wire brush.

6.9 The hubs can be difficult to polish properly, but, by using a small multi-tool with a polishing head, you can get into more inaccessible areas.

6.7 When refitting the brake shoes, apply a little grease to the brake cam. This one is very dry.

6.10 Polishing the difficult areas with a multi-tool.

6.11 After a short time: a nicely-polished hub.

optimum handling performance. The motorcycle manufacturer will have a recommended tyre, and there is likely to be a modern equivalent for the bike if the original is no longer available.

Always fit new inner tubes when fitting new tyres. An old inner tube will be stretched, and can crease and fail due to the thin rubber.

It is possible to change or fit tyres yourself using tyre levers, but, if your project has been unused for some time, you will find that the rubber has gone very hard and is almost impossible to remove by yourself. Take the wheels to the motorcycle shop where you're buying the new tyres – the staff will fit the tyres for free. This is the best option, because they'll balance the wheels at the same time, something you can't do at home.

Once the old tyre is removed, it's very likely that the inside of the rim (under the inner tube) will have some areas of rust. The tyre fitter uses a wire brush to remove these, then fits rim tape, which covers the heads of the spokes, so that should rust re-appear, it will not cause a puncture.

Here (photo 6.14), the fitter is about to fit the new Bridgestone tyre to the wheel. With the wheel tightly clamped to the machine, the tyre is easier to fit.

TYRES

Tyres are an essential part of a motorcycle, and must be in good condition for your own safety. In competition terms, worn tyres will struggle to compete against tyres in better condition. If there are signs of perishing, low tread, splits and cuts, the tyre should be changed.

I have never had a restoration project where the tyres were in good enough condition to re-use. Always allow for a new set of tyres on your project, and don't forget to include the inner tubes and rim tape, too, if they are not the tubeless sort.

Tyres should be changed in pairs, and be from the same manufacturer. The tyres are designed to work together as a pair to keep

6.12 A tyre showing clear signs of perishing. This is dangerous: if the tyre is worn, or looks like this, renew it.

6.13 After 20 years on the wheel, the old tyre had be taken to a tyre workshop to be removed.

6.14 Wheels tightly clamped, and new rim tape fitted. The tape prevents the spoke heads touching the inner tube.

6.15 Make sure that the fitter knows the direction of rotation of the wheel. It's not obvious, and must be pointed out before a new tyre is fitted.

Be sure to find out the correct pressures for your bike's tyres, and frequently check that the tyres are at this level. This is the most important tyre maintenance function you can perform. They must be inflated to the correct pressure for your safety and competitiveness.

Use a good quality gauge that holds a reading, especially before a competition.

6.16 Lastly, the essential tyre pressure check. It's important to use the correct tyre pressures, or safety and early wear problems can arise.

6.17 Time to go now; other customers are waiting.

6.18 Finished wheel and tyre combination, cleaned, re-painted, and with new rubber. The tyres will need approximately 100km, or 60 miles, scrubbing in before they reach optimum performance.

Chapter 7
Fuel & exhaust systems

At this stage, it's time to take a close look at the fuel and exhaust system. Blockages in either will result in poor running, or not running at all. The vast majority of problems are likely to come from a fuel blockage, but a heavily coked exhaust will reduce performance (this is more common on two-stroke models, but worth checking on any motorcycle).

FUEL TANK

The fuel tank is one place you really do not want *any* rust or scale. Even small particles will cause running problems, blocking the filters in the fuel tap, or carburettor.

Rust remover can be used effectively on the inside of the fuel tank, followed by a resin fuel tank liner, if necessary. An alloy or plastic/fibreglass fuel tank will be much less likely to have a bad contamination problem.

Fuel tanks often have rust, scale, or even old fuel that has turned to sludge at the bottom. This will need to be thoroughly cleaned out before adding fuel again.

If the tank is more seriously contaminated, it will need further cleaning.

7.1 If the inside of the tank looks like this, it will need attention before you can add fuel.

7.2 This slim Yamaha TY tank shows only slight rusting, and requires just a light clean. Rinse out the tank with a small amount of two-stroke oil/fuel mix. Swill it around, so the fuel reaches all parts of the tank, then empty into a suitable container. This will clear out particles, and the two-stroke mixture will help prevent formation of further rust.

Begin by removing the fuel tap, setting it aside for a closer inspection later. There are various ways to clean the inside of the tank. If it has sludge and scale, place a few handfuls of small gravel – the type used in aquariums, that you can find in a local pet shop – in the tank, and shake. This helps to abrade the inside, and loosen the encrusted debris.

Find something to block the fuel tap hole (a piece of cork from a wine bottle will do): you do not want the rust-removing fluid to leak out. Next, rinse the tank with warm soapy water. Then empty the water, and dry. Finally, add the rust-remover solution.

When the rust-removing process is complete, dry the tank thoroughly. I place the tank on a small oil-filled radiator at a low heat setting for a few hours to make sure it's 100 per cent dry inside. You can also use a hair dryer to blow warm air through the tank. Whichever method you use, the tank needs to be completely dry.

A clean tank will rust very quickly if not dried or protected soon. If the tank was in particularly bad condition, you may want to consider lining it with a resin-based tank sealer. These also bind together rust or scale that could not be removed, and can fill tiny pin holes that may be present.

While the tank is clean and empty of fuel, this is the stage to carry out cosmetic work (see Chapter 8).

If the tank wasn't in bad condition, and once the fuel tap is re-fitted, you can add some petrol with a small amount of two-stroke oil. Give it a light swill around, and the oil will coat the sides of the tank and prevent rust reforming. You can use this method even if your bike is a four-stroke.

Set the tank aside until later.

FUEL TAP

With the wide range of off-road models now classed as classics, there is also a wide assortment of fuel taps and carburettors. For detailed information of your particular model you will need the specific manual that goes with it. The steps of the strip down and rebuild shown here are applicable, even if your particular carb or tap is different to the one shown.

Dismantle the fuel tap, being careful not to lose small parts, such as springs, screws, etc.

When dismantling the fuel tap or carburettor, try not to tear the gaskets or seals. It's most likely and recommended that you replace all of them with new parts, but, if they are not freely available, you may be able to re-use one or two that you have removed.

The fuel taps and carburettors can often be seized solid, and will need some gentle persuasion to release them. Use light oil, and let it soak for a while to penetrate into the threads and joints before attempting to unscrew anything. If the part is really stuck firm, you could immerse it in hot water for a few minutes; then try again – be careful not to scald yourself.

7.3 Unscrew the fuel tap from the tank, and put away the screws somewhere safe for use later. Any washers present are likely to need replacement. You will find at least one O-ring, or other rubber seal, between the fuel tap and the tank. This is also likely to need replacement.

7.4 Once the fuel tap is detached, place it on a clean surface ready for dismantling. A small amount of fuel is likely to spill when you remove the bowl, so it's a good idea to have some clean cloth ready to wipe it up.

7.5 Unscrew the fuel tap bowl. Be prepared for some fuel to spill out.

7.6 It's normal to find particles in the bowl. Note the condition of the rubber seal – save if undamaged.

7.7 Once the bowl is removed, you will see the fuel tap filter. Remove gently, clean with carburettor cleaner, and blow through with an airline.

7.8 and 7.9 With the majority of fuel taps, remove the tap arm by unscrewing the faceplate screws. Sometimes, as with the small Yamaha tap in photo 7.9, the arm is held in place by a single screw on the side of the tap body.

7.10 Once the face plate is removed, there will often be a light spring that keeps the tap arm firm when in use.

7.11 and 7.12 Here, you can see the fuel tap's rubber seal. Gently prise this out using a small screwdriver or similar, trying not to split the seal: it may come in useful later.

7.13 Now, only the fuel tap body is left. Once dismantled, you will be able to see the passages through which fuel should flow. Every passageway should be cleaned thoroughly. Using an airline, try to blow through the passages. If they are completely blocked, you'll need a small pointed object, such as a watchmaker's screwdriver, to gently dig out the scale and push through. Once the passages are nearly clear, use carburettor cleaner to remove 'varnish' deposits.

7.14 and 7.15 Ideally, this is the point at which you would use an ultrasonic cleaner. Small ones are inexpensive and suitable for cleaning smaller items. When cleaning larger parts, such as the carburettor body, you will need a larger model. If you do not have an ultrasonic cleaner, use carburettor cleaner and a small pointed tool to release deposits.

If the seals and gaskets came out in one piece, it may be possible to reuse them, but it's always best to fit a rebuild kit, if you can find one.

CARBURETTOR

This section shows the strip down and rebuild of a Amal Mk2 carburettor, which was used on lots of motorcycles, with some references to a Yamaha TY carburettor, comparable to many used on Japanese models. The components are similar to most other carburettors, with only minor differences between makes and models. The workshop manual will give more detail on your specific one.

When dismantling, it's a good idea to take photos, and notes, so you know where the parts go when you come to rebuilding.

The carburettor has to be immaculately clean inside. There are small fuel and air passages that are tiny, and can easily become clogged. On all projects, I would recommend a full strip down and rebuild of the carburettors, unless the bike was running very nicely when you bought it.

The carburettor is connected to the cylinder in various ways: some connectors are rubber, some a rubber/alloy combination, others alloy only. If you have a rubber connection, check for splits or perishing. If the rubbers are damaged, they'll need to be replaced.

7.16 When everything is cleaned, rebuild the fuel tap in reverse order of dismantling. Once fitted, it should work like new.

7.17 Start by removing the air filter. Then disconnect all cables and fuel pipes, leaving only the carburettor and rubbers to be removed.

7.18 On this model, Montesa used a rubber-only connection between carburettor and cylinder manifold. These often get very hard over the years and become more like plastic. Loosen the clamps on the rubber connector and carefully pull off the carburettor, followed by the rubber connector itself.

7.20 This carb is connected to the cylinder by an all-alloy reed valve block.

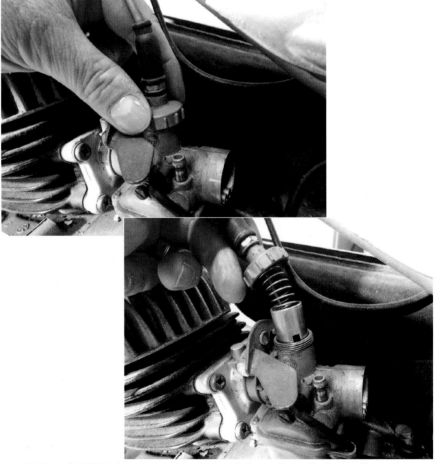

7.19 On alloy/rubber combinations, be very careful when trying to remove carburettors from a motorcycle that has not been used for years – the rubber can break away from the alloy, making the small manifold unusable. This type also uses a rubber O-ring seal, which must be replaced.

7.21 and 7.22 Before removing the carb from the cylinder, pull out the carburettor slide. Unscrew the knurled top and lift out the slide.

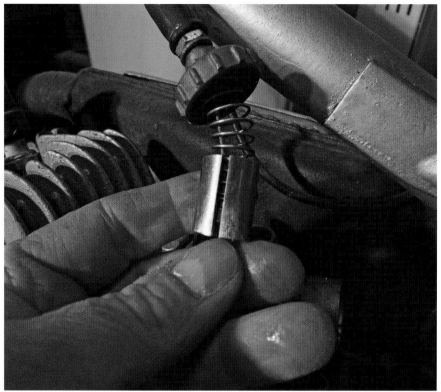

7.23 Note the slot in the carburettor slide. This locates on a peg inside the carburettor body, to ensure the slide is fitted facing in the correct direction.

7.24 Simply unscrew the clamp's bolt and twist off the carburettor.

Once removed, place the carburettor on a very clean work area, ready to be dismantled.

Tip: Twin carbs. Use a small clean plastic container (margarine tub) for each carburettor. When

7.25 Before you begin to dismantle the carb, drain any fuel that is in its bowl. On most carbs, there is a drain screw, or bolt, at the bottom of the bowl. Unscrew this over a container to catch the fuel.

7.26 If there is no drain screw on the bowl, place the overflow pipes in a suitable jar and tip the carb until fuel runs out.

dismantling, place all the pieces from one carb in one container, thus keeping each carb's parts separate.

Clean the main body of the carb to remove dirt and grime before dismantling. This will help to keep the inside clean when it's dismantled.

7.27 Remove the fuel filter housing.

7.28 With the housing free, the fuel filter will become visible.

7.29 Remove the filter and clean with carburettor cleaner.

7.30 Remove the bowl of the carburettor, by unscrewing the (usually) four screws. Try not to damage the bowl's gasket. The fuel remaining will run out, so have a container ready. Remember, no naked flames!

7.31 Once the bowl is off, take a look inside. This one has the fuel float and float needle inside. Often, the bowl is empty, with the float and needle in the main body of the carburettor.

7.32 Remove the gasket so that the float pivot pin is now visible ...

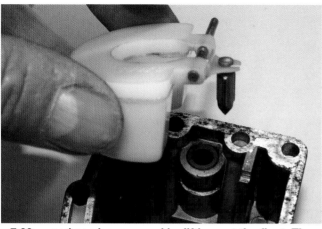

7.33 ... and can be removed by lifting out the float. The needle just sits lightly in the float, so be careful that it does not drop out and become lost.

7.36 A float, as used in a Yamaha TY carburettor.

7.34 A more common arrangement is shown here, with the float removed by pushing out the metal pin, using a small pointed object. The pin normally pushes out quite easily.

7.37 Visible inside this carburettor, from a Yamaha TY model: the needle jet, main jet, pilot jet, float needle valve and its seal.

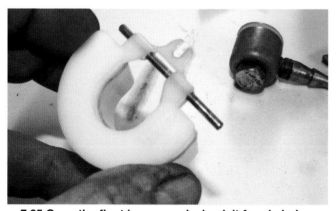

7.35 Once the float is removed, check it for pin holes. Hold it under warm water: if there are holes, bubbles will appear, in which case, it will need to be replaced – unless it's a brass float, which can be repaired with a small spot of solder.

7.38 Jets are removed by using small spanners and screwdriver.

7.39 Replace fibre washers that look damaged.

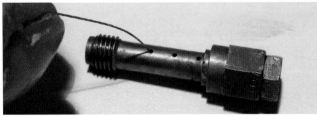

7.40 Particles that are firmly stuck will need to be pushed out with a piece of wire. Also flush with carburettor cleaner to remove fine deposits.

7.41 Remove the air screw and clean it with carburettor cleaner. Before doing so, tighten it with a screwdriver until it is fully screwed in, noting how many complete turns you have made. When replacing the air screw, screw it in fully, and then unscrew it by the number of turns noted before. This will help to achieve a basic fuel air mixture setting.

7.42 Remove the tickover adjustment screw (clean with carburettor cleaner), followed by the choke mechanism.

7.43 With this Amal Mk2 carburettor fully dismantled, we can now thoroughly clean all components, along with the main body, inside and out.

7.44 Rebuild in the reverse order of dismantling, using thoroughly cleaned or new parts.

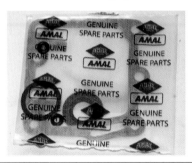

7.45 I recommend that a carburettor rebuild kit be fitted – a genuine one, if possible, but aftermarket kits are usually okay. This is a gasket kit for a Amal Mk2 carburettor.

Fitting new fuel and overflow pipes, and an inline fuel filter, is recommended.

Once the carbs are rebuilt, set the float height and jets according to the workshop manual. Now place the carbs in a clean container out of the way (so no dust can contaminate them), ready for refitting.

EXHAUST SYSTEM

The exhaust system is often in poor condition, with rust holes and dented or scratched chrome. It's also one of the most difficult parts to find in good condition secondhand, and not easy to find new at all for older motorcycles. Most aftermarket exhaust systems are very good – better than the original exhaust would have been. This is particularly so for the Pre '65 models, but they can also be very expensive. If you do not necessarily want the bike to be 100% original, there are lots of easy-to-source off-the-shelf generic silencer options open to you.

Acids and water generated by combustion can lead to holes developing in the exhaust silencer: any holes found will require a braze repair, if a replacement silencer is not available (or necessary).

7.47 Accident damage caused during bike events is often seen on exhaust systems. This is type of damage is repairable, if necessary.

7.46 This Ariel has a good example of an aftermarket off-road exhaust system, with a small alloy silencer fitted.

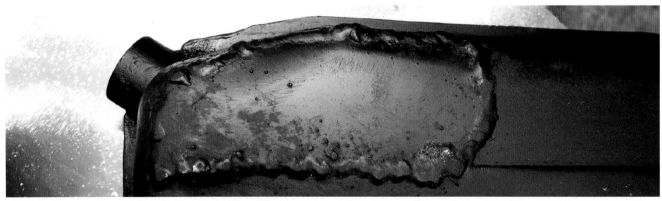

7.48 If damage is on the unseen underside of the exhaust, and is not a split or a hole, the bike could be ridden until a replacement is found. The silencer illustrated has an old welded repair; ugly, but it's out of sight, and does not affect the sound or performance of the bike.

7.48a It's likely that the exhaust system is at least a little rusty: if it's not too bad, the rust can be sanded off, and the exhaust, if painted, can be repainted.

7.48c Use a high temperature spray paint for the exhaust.

7.48b Sand the exhaust components to remove rust.

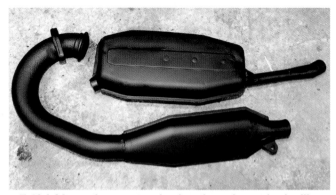

7.48d After a few coats of paint, the exhaust looks like new.

There is very little maintenance required on the exhaust system, other than keeping it clean and clear of carbon deposits – less of a problem on four-strokes, than on two-, where carbon can quickly build up from two-stroke oil smoke. When this occurs, the baffles need to be removed and cleaned. The baffle wadding should be replaced, too, if it's damaged.

7.49 The tail pipe on this two-stroke's silencer is clearly oiled up, and will require cleaning.

7.52 Once the baffles are out use a small wire brush and some degreaser to remove the carbon. The heat-resistant wadding is missing from this baffle and will require replacing.

7.50 In order to remove and clean the baffles follow the instructions in your bike's workshop manual. However, usually, there is a small hole, often on the underside of the exhaust, inside which is either a screw or a bolt holding the baffle in place.

7.53 Sheets of baffle wadding are inexpensive and easy to cut to size with a pair of scissors.

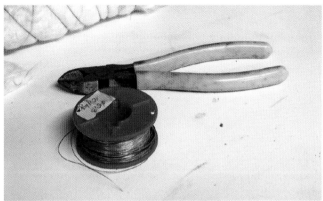

7.54 You will need a pair of wire cutters and some wire.

7.51 Remove the screw or bolt, and pull out the baffle with a suitable pair of pliers. The baffles are quite long. Twisting the baffle from side to side, while pulling, will help to release it, and loosen carbon holding it back.

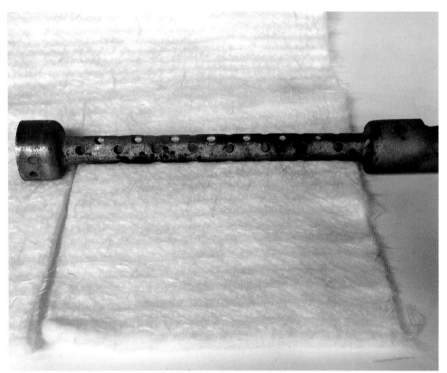

Check for cracks and holes in the exhaust system. Their presence is likely to lead to failure of a roadworthiness test. Check all joints for exhaust gas leaks. Gaskets and exhaust seals are usually available for joints and connecting to the cylinder head. Where possible, it's advisable to renew seals between joints, if they are leaking.

7.55 These baffles have been cleaned, with all the holes now visible. Place on the wadding to measure the correct size.

7.58 The exhaust seal in the cylinder/ cylinder head is usually a large crush-type washer, made of copper or aluminium. This should always be replaced with a new item.

7.56 Roll the wadding tightly around the baffle ...

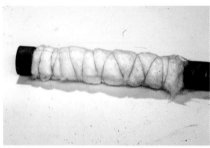

7.57 ... and secure tightly with the wire. Use the scissors to trim excess wadding. The baffle is now ready to be re-fitted to the exhaust.

7.59 Original exhaust systems are hard to find in good condition, but this one has survived – largely because the majority of it is well hidden, out of harm's way.

Chapter 8
Paint spraying & decals

Many parts on your off-road project would originally have been painted or lacquered. After all this time, they'll almost certainly be scratched – at the very least, they'll have faded over the years. In this chapter, we will go through the process of re-spraying and restoring them to their original finish.

8.1 This Yamaha TY175 has great paintwork and decals, demonstrating what can be achieved by respraying bodywork and replacing decals. The tank and side panels/heat shield are conspicuous, but parts such as fork legs are often forgotten. Some will be polished, others painted. (Courtesy Robbie Rogers)

Here is a list of parts that are usually painted or powdercoated:

- Fuel tank
- Side panels or heat shield
- Frame
- Swinging arm
- Sidestand
- Exhaust
- Engine & cylinder head
- Foot rest brackets
- Top and bottom yokes
- Rear torque arm
- Air filter box
- Fork legs
- Headlamp cowl
- Speedo housing
- Seat base
- Engine mounting brackets

8.3 A wide range of paint shop products is required to complete the project. Motorcycle parts are generally small, so, if you don't have spray equipment, a spray can should produce a good result.

As you can see, a considerable number of parts require painting if you want your bike to look as good as new. The method of preparation and painting is the same, whatever you're intending to respray. Tip: If the part has decals, note where they are placed. You may want to take photos for reference later. It could be useful to take measurements of the current decals, so you can refer to them when you're attaching the new ones, after repainting (see photos 8.21-8.23 on pages 91-92).

Firstly, remember, fumes from thinners and paints are dangerous and highly flammable. Two Pack paint should only be used by professionals, with the appropriate safety equipment, although it's more durable and can be polished to a higher shine than other paints. Aerosol and cellulose paints are more suitable for DIY use. Do not use near flames or sparks, and wear the appropriate face mask at all times. Speak to your paint provider, if you're not sure which mask to use.

Likewise, when sanding, use an appropriate dust particle mask, as sanding dust can damage your health.

Tools and materials you will require:

Preparation
- Sander
- Filler
- Cellulose
- Putty
- Wet and dry paper (grades 120, 240, 500)
- Dust particle mask
- Degreaser

Priming
- Spray aerosol primer, or compressor and spray gun
- Primer
- Thinners
- Tack cloth
- Spray mask
- Strainer (if using a spray gun)

Finish coat
- Same tools as for priming
- Finish paint
- 1200 grade wet and dry paper
- Polishing compound

Let's start with the fuel tank. This is often the main focus of attention and must look good.

Once the tank is cleaned inside and completely empty of fuel, as described in Chapter 7, remove the fuel tap, cap and all badges or decals, so that all you have is a completely bare tank.

There are many paint suppliers

8.2 The whole frame on this later Husqvarna 250 is sprayed white, including the fork legs and rear shocks.

8.4 Remove all badges and decals prior to spray preparation.

that will mix the colour that you require and send it to you in an aerosol. Because the area that requires spraying on a motorcycle is relatively small, this does not always justify buying spray equipment. I will assume that you will be using spray cans but If you have spray equipment the process is the same.

STRIPPING PAINT/APPLYING NEW PAINT

Preparation is paramount and will reflect in the finished paint surface quality. With parts in a very bad condition, for instance, the fuel tank, it's worth spending the extra time and strip it back to the bare metal (later model bikes often used a plastic or fibreglass fuel tank. Do not use paint stripper on plastic or fibreglass parts). Preparing for painting over badly adhering paint

8.5 Automotive paint strippers are available for removing old paint from car body panels. These are suitable for paint removal from metal bike parts that require repainting.

may take just as long and results will be far from perfect.

Chemical strippers are very strong, so the manufacturers' safety instructions must be followed correctly. Gloves, goggles and good ventilation are essential.

For a painted metal fuel tank, the process for stripping parts is as follows.

8.6 Lightly brush the stripper onto the part to be stripped. After a short while, the paint starts to bubble and blister. Once the whole part has been covered with stripper, you can begin to scrape off the paint, using a paint scraper.

8.7 This will remove almost all the paint. Some difficult-to-reach areas may require another coat, and you can get to inaccessible crevices by using a small wire brush or some wire wool.

Next, wash the part thoroughly with water (this neutralises the stripper) and dry it.

8.8 If you have a plastic or fibreglass tank, sand the area to be sprayed, prior to applying the first coat of primer.

8.9 Once sanded, dents and scratches will be more clearly visible.

8.10 Once the part is dry, take a closer look at it. If there are dents, these will require filling to return the tank to its original shape.

8.11 After a few coats of primer, small imperfections, that still require filling and rubbing down, will be easier to see.

8.12 After the first coat of primer, sand the tank again and fill small imperfections with a fine surface filler.

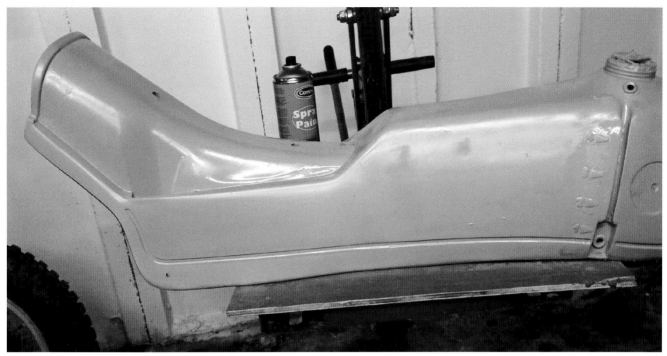

8.13 This tank has been completely sanded, with dents filled. Dry it thoroughly and then spray the first coat of primer. Follow the instructions on the can. Spaying must be carried out in a well-ventilated area using the appropriate safety mask and goggles. Spray fumes should not be inhaled, so use a face mask.

You will need a two-part car body filler. Follow the instructions, and smooth the filler into the dent, leaving it slightly proud of the tank surface.

If the dent is large, it will require building up with more than one layer of filler. Once you have filled all the dents, let the filler harden. Then begin to sand the filled areas with wet and dry abrasive paper (use a dust mask and goggles here). Start with a reasonably coarse grade of 120 just to get the shape. You may find a rubber sanding block makes this easier. Keep the paper wrapped around it. Once you have sanded to the shape required, you will need to go over again with progressively finer and finer grades of wet and dry. After grade 120, use 240, 500, and finish with 1200. Make sure you keep the wet and dry paper wet when sanding. This helps prevent it becoming clogged with old paint residue.

8.14 Find a solid platform on which to place the part to be sprayed, or, even better, hang it on a piece of strong cord or wire, as with this swing arm. This will allow you to spray all sides, top, and underneath without moving it.

If you can't hang the tank, spray the underneath first. Once that's completely dry, turn it over and spray the top and sides. Make sure you allow the primer and finish paint to completely dry between coats. If the paint is still slightly wet and you apply more paint, runs will occur, and you will have to begin again, rubbing these out.

8.15 Use fine surface body filler and go over with a fine wet and dry sandpaper, keeping it wet until the area is smooth again. Now re-apply two more coats of primer.

You will need to continue this process until there are no imperfections, and the tank is completely smooth and fully primed.

If you come across very small scratches or dents you can use more fine filler or cellulose putty. This is applied lightly with a small plastic spatula and pressed into the scratches or dents. It usually dries quite quickly.

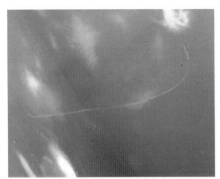

8.16 Here you can see a scratch, filled with fine cellulose putty.

Now that you have the tank 100% smooth and fully primed, you can move onto the finish coats.

Carefully wipe the tank using a tack cloth to remove fine dust from the area to be sprayed.

8.17 Spray two to three coats of finish paint, and let it dry completely between coats. Examine the surface carefully. Has it picked up dust while spraying? Are there runs? Is the paint texture a little like orange peel? Any of these will mean another rub over with a fine grade wet and dry paper.

If you're happy with the results, pat yourself on the back, well done. It's not easy the first time and if you have a good result now, results will only get better in the future.

Don't worry too much if it's not 100%. It's your first attempt. Runs, dust and the orange peel effect are common and can all be dealt with. If you do have runs, you will have to rub down the affected areas lightly, and respray.

The orange peel effect can be flattened with a very fine, wet and dry paper when the paint has cured. Leave as long as recommended by the manufacturer. The paint must have hardened fully before you can start cutting back.

After a few attempts, you will have a finished tank with no blemishes. If the paint you use is a metallic one, it will require two coats of lacquer to get the final shine. Lacquer can also be flattened and polished, but, as with the top coat, leave until the lacquer has hardened fully.

Once the last coats are hardened, whether lacquer or paint, go over the whole tank with a fine rubbing compound or 2000 grit paper and a soft block, until you have a high shine.

Whenever you rub down or polish. ensure that the surface is completely free from particles that could cause scratches to the finished work.

8.18 Don't forget to paint the smaller parts, such as the stand, brackets and levers. These can all be painted the same way as the tank.

Once the spraying is finished, it's time to turn your attention to the badges and decals, to finish off the appearance of the bike.

DECALS

All motorcycles have decals. They give the manufacturer's name and sometimes the model's, too. Some are decorative, such as pinstriping; others are for information, such as tyre pressure and other safety warnings stickers. To make the bike look as original as possible, try to locate the decals for your model. Some are still available, but many have been discontinued. Don't worry: help is at hand. There are many decal companies that reproduce exact replicas. Most decals are small stickers that peel off a backing paper, and are simply stuck to the bike. With vinyl decals, technique is more important, as it can be quite challenging to get them right.

8.19 A variety of sticker decals: these are for a Honda road model, but the warning and caution stickers are very similar to those found on off-road models.

There are two main methods of applying decals – the wet method and the dry method. Both are basically the same procedure, but using the wet method does give a little more time for final positioning.

The main rules

- Do a practice run first: position the decal without sticking it, so you have a basic idea of where you're going to position it.
- Relax, take your time: if you rush you will make mistakes.

Here are the tools you will require:

- Craft knife
- Small garden sprayer
- Lint-free cloth

8.20 The stripes do not look much to start with, and arrive either folded or rolled up. Unfold and place them on a flat surface: this helps flatten out creases, and prevents decals lifting when applied to the bike.

8.21 Try to find a fixed point to measure from. If you can't, use a piece of card as seen here. The measurements recorded can be referred to when you're ready to apply stripes.

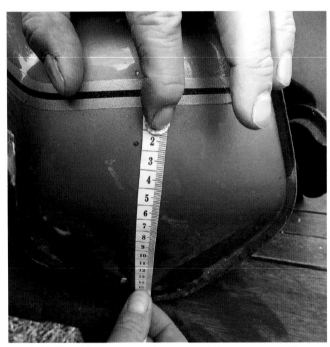

8.22 If you have more than one stripe, measure the distance between them; write down all measurements taken.

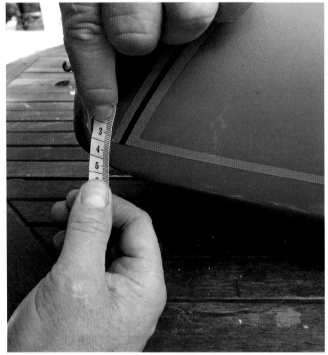

8.23 Take plenty of measurements. The more you take, the more accurate the new stripe will be.

Before you remove the backing paper, cut it as close as you can to the decal, making sure not to damage it.
Add a couple of drops of washing up liquid to the garden sprayer and then fill with cold water. Two drops will be enough. Lightly spray the solution onto the tank.

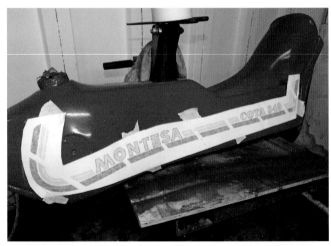

8.24 Lightly spray the tank with water, and position the stripes gently on the tank. Then, with a pencil, make small marks on the tank to highlight the points that you measured. This will help keep the decal in the right position. Use masking tape to hold the decal in position.

8.25 Next, remove the backing paper from the decal and carefully stick it onto the tank using the pencil lines as a guide. Now press the decal firmly all over. Be careful not to stretch or scratch it.

Lastly, peel off the top layer of paper to reveal the finished stripe.

8.26 Wipe with a lint-free cloth to dry the area, and to make sure that the decal is firmly fixed to the tank.

If you have two stripes, overlap them at the corner, and trim with a craft knife to a clean edge.

8.27 Now to the badges: this type has a sticky glue backing.

8.28 Offer the badge into place. Once you're happy with the position, press firmly so that it sticks well.

8.30 This is one of my favourite decals, from a 1969 Greeves Griffon 380. Some classics have more elaborate and decorative badges, mostly made of metal, alloy or plastic. Raised embossed types are very attractive, too.

8.29 That's it: you have just applied your own decal; more money saved. With a couple of coats of lacquer, this tank will look like new.

A set of badges in original condition can fetch a good price on auction websites, because they are becoming more and more difficult to find in good condition.

Some are reproduced and available, but often the reproductions are of poor quality. I have come across ones that don't fit the locating holes on the side panels, leaving the buyer having to cut off the locating pins and glue the badge in position.

This is not what you should have to do when you've just paid good money for a new part.

You can have some success restoring badges, particularly if they are metal or alloy.

8.31 What a well turned out Bultaco Pursang 360 scrambler: resprayed and with new decals and badges, and looking very smart. Not just for show, this bike's performance was as good as its looks on the day!

VISIT VELOCE ON THE WEB – WWW.VELOCE.CO.UK
All current books • New book news • Special offers • Gift vouchers • Forum

94

Chapter 9
Seat

On a finished project, it's essential that the seat looks and feels right – however, with almost all restoration projects, it needs work. The cover can split or tear, due to the constant change between cold and warm weather over a long period of time, or as a result of being leaned against a wall or shed. The foam is susceptible to deterioration, too.

Seats can be recovered, and, where splits/tears are not too large, the foam underneath may be in usable condition.

9.1 Old seat foam is not often completely unusable, but exposure to sunlight can cause severe deterioration, as here.

Foam is an easy material to work with, and, if you only have a small repair, it's quite simple to cut a piece and fix it to a damaged area with a little glue. The seat cover, when fitted, will be tight and help hold the repair in place. However, if the foam has been exposed for too long, it will have deteriorated too much to be repairable, and a complete new seat foam will be required.

Seat covers are available for most models, but there are different styles for each year of production or model type – later trials bikes have tiny seats; in contrast, earlier models had a seat of a similar size to that of road models. Try to get the correct style for your bike. Motorcycle seat covers are not difficult to fit, and are relatively inexpensive to purchase, too.

If the seat cover requires renewal, ensure that you order the exact seat cover for the motorcycle model, year and type. I once ordered a seat cover for a Honda 1973 CB350T – only slightly different from my model, a 1973 CB350F, but I had to buy a second cover, after the first one ripped while I was trying to 'make it fit.' Lesson learnt.

9.2 The worst problems you can have on a seat involve the seat base, most of which are made of pressed metal. They rust over the years, and a badly corroded base can often be beyond repair. In order to secure the seat to the bike, the hinges and brackets must be sound, and firmly attached to the base. If they aren't, you will have to find a way to repair them, or you will need to replace it.

9.3 A seat base like this is too badly corroded to be repaired. You can see that the edge of the seat base has completely rusted away. Small holes can be covered by a plate riveted to the base, giving some strength to that area, but more serious damage means another base will be required.

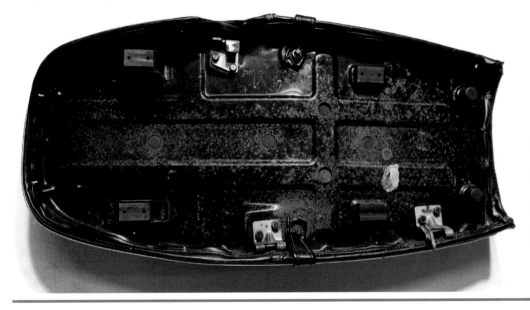

9.4 This base is in good condition, showing only light rust. It's complete, with the hinges and catches solidly attached. Also visible are the seat rubbers that support the seat on the motorcycle frame. There are six on this seat base.

9.5 This little Honda CR125 Elsinore has a seat as large as that of a road bike of the same period.

9.6 This seat will require recovering; luckily, it has no foam damage at all, so should be a straightforward cover replacement.

9.7 This seat is part of a seat/tank all-in-one unit. Turn it upside down, and undo the two nuts.

9.8 Now lift free the seat.

9.9 The base of this seat is in relatively good condition, but the cover is completely glued in position. This works well on a smaller seat, but larger ones require metal clasps to hold the cover in position.

The following sections show gluing and fixing with metal clasps, and should cover almost all types of seat.

Seat covers that are glued

9.10 The glue has failed in some areas on this seat.

9.11 Peel back the seat cover, working around the edges, and remove it completely.

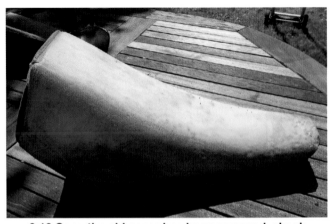

9.12 Once the old cover has been removed, check the foam for damage or deterioration. This foam is in reasonably good condition for its age.

9.13 Use a wire brush to remove rust.

9.14 Once the rust has been removed, spray the rusted area with an all-in-one paint, such as Hammerite Smooth, which doesn't require priming. This will give a strong base for the glue to adhere to. It doesn't have to look perfect: you're just trying to provide a clean surface for the glue.

9.15 The new seat cover, ready to be fitted.

9.16 Pull the seat cover over the front of the seat.

9.17 Next, pull the back of the cover over the seat foam.

9.18 Pull both sides down evenly. If there are contours or lines, make sure they are level with each other.

9.19 Now, check the underside of the seat to see that the cover sits evenly all the way around.

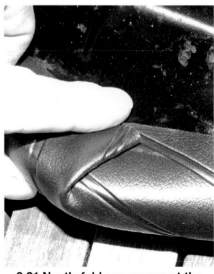

9.21 Neatly fold any excess at the corners, and glue this, too.

9.22 Find some way to hold the cover while the glue dries. I used a small clamp, but only applied very light pressure – just enough to keep it tight.

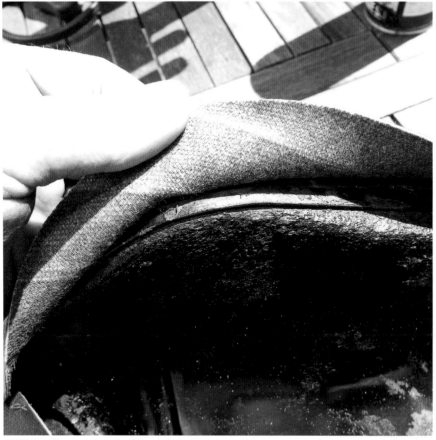

9.20 Apply glue to all of the fabric – ensure the type you choose is suitable for gluing the material to the metal base.

9.23 Once you have glued all the way around, and the glue is dry, the seat will look like new, and be ready for fitting.

Seats with metal clasps

9.24 Gently prise off the edge strip fasteners from the underside of the seat.

9.25 Give a light tap with a hammer to loosen the pins, and then pull them out.

9.26 The seat has metal clasps and hooks all around the inside edge of the base. These hold the seat cover tight in place. Often these clasps are broken or rusted away. This one is in good condition. Bend them up to release the cover.

9.27 If the seat has a strap fitted, this will need to be removed to allow the seat cover to come off. Start by detaching the spring clips.

9.28 Now, unbolt all the brackets and hinges, ready for degreasing and painting.

9.29 The smaller clasps are not so easy to get at with pliers, so you'll require a flat blade screwdriver or similar to prise them up.

9.32 Work across the front of the seat, until all the pointed clasps are through, and bend them all so that they hold the seat cover in position.

9.30 Pull the edge trim off the seat, working all the way around the base, until the cover can be removed completely.

Follow the procedure for cleaning the seat base as described for the glued seat.

Do the same at the back, and all around the edges, too.

It's possible that original seat clasps have rusted and may even have snapped. They could break off while you're trying to straighten them, when removing the seat cover. The following procedure is a reliable method of replacing the clasps to enable you to fit the new seat cover.

9.33 Metal clasp kits (seat spikes) are available, and are very good for replacing either the original broken clasps, or for fitting to a fibreglass seat.

Note: Be aware that these spikes are very sharp and care must be taken when handling them.

9.34 You will require a small rivet gun and some rivets ...

9.35 ... and a pair of tin snips, to cut the seat spike strips to length.

9.31 Now, with the cover pulled tightly at the front, pierce it with the pointed clasps.

9.36 Measure the length of spike strip required, and cut to size.

9.39 ... continuing until the spikes go around the whole seat edge.

9.37 To rivet the spikes to the seat, first drill holes round the seat edge, placing the spike strip in position and drilling through the holes in the strip. Use the correct drill bit for the rivets.

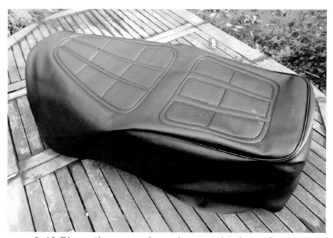

9.40 Place the cover loosely over the foam base.

9.38 Then, rivet the spikes to the seat edge ...

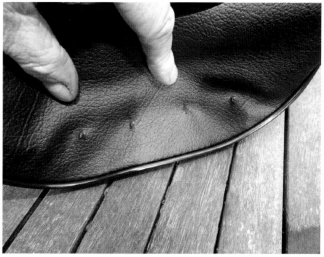

9.41 Pull the front and back of the cover, so that the seat cover edging lines up with the profile of the seat. Do this on both sides, so that the seat pattern is central to the top of the seat.

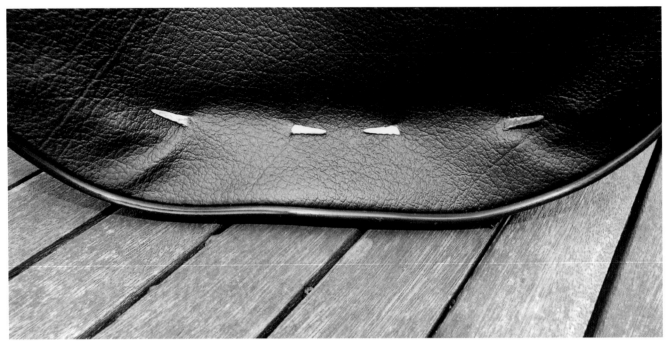

9.42 Bend back the spikes as shown.

9.43 Work around the front of the seat, until all the spikes are through, and bend each one, so that they all hold the seat cover in position.

Finally, cut off excess material with a sharp knife.

Chapter 10
Forks

Motorcycle manufacturers have devised various kinds of front suspension, the vast majority of which comprise telescopic forks with hydraulic damping. This chapter covers the stripping and rebuilding of front forks of this kind, since it's the type that you're most likely to come across on your off-road project.

Before you attempt to rebuild the forks, check for scratches on the stanchions. These cause damage to the fork oil seal, and, if present, mean the stanchions must be reground and plated by a specialist company. It's pointless fitting new seals if this hasn't been carried out beforehand: the seal will simply fail again. You will still have to strip the forks in order to send the stanchions for refurbishment.

It's common, too, for fork oil to leak, or break down, so it must be replaced. Drain the old oil (photo 10.2), and, using the correct grade of oil, top up to the right level. This is usually a measured amount (see your workshop manual), when filling the forks.

The main components of the front forks are as follows.

10.1 The fork leg, which will be polished, is the part that the stanchions slide into. On most motorcycles this comprises the bottom part of the forks, although later, mainly on sports models, it was the upper part, known as upside-down forks (USD).

10.2 When the fork oil requires changing, it's drained from a removable screw like the example that can be seen here.

10.3 The stanchion: this is chrome-plated and slides into the fork leg. If it is scratched, it will damage the seal and lead to an oil leak. The stanchion often has a cover, in the form of either a rubber gaiter or a painted metal shroud, to protect it.

10.6 Oily residue is a sign that a fork leg is leaking. The oil seal will need to be replaced.

10.4 A close-up of this stanchion shows rust and pit marks. It will have to be re-ground and chrome-plated, before the fork leg can be rebuilt.

10.7 Drain any oil in the forks, either through the small screw at the bottom of the fork leg, or by turning it upside down. Place a container (not glass) under the fork leg and drain the oil. (You may have to compress the fork a little to expel the oil – so a glass container would break.)

10.5 The coil spring can become compressed over time, and will have to be checked against the manufacturer's measurements to see if it's still the correct length to be used. The correct length of spring will be found in the workshop manual.

10.8 Next, remove the dust cover by prising it out of its slot and sliding it off the top of the fork leg.

10.9 Now we can see the circlip in the top of the fork leg. Clean away rust.

10.10 Holding the leg firmly, remove the circlip and give it a good clean.

10.11 There is a bolt (sometimes a screw) on the underside of the fork leg that must be removed now …

10.12 … this bolt/screw is often very tight, and may never have been removed before. It's important to use the correct size screwdriver or Allen key: if it becomes rounded, it will be very difficult to remove because of its location. Try shocking the screw before attempting to turn it, to help break the adhesion.

10.13 Remove the oil seal, making sure you do not damage the inner face of the stanchion.

10.14 Withdraw the stanchion. Sometimes a slide hammer action is required here.

10.15 Once out, the spring will become visible. Be prepared for more oil to spill out at this point.

10.16 Clean the damper rod thoroughly.

10.17 All visible holes must be clear of debris.

10.18 Slightly grease the stanchion before refitting the top bush to the forks.

10.19 Clean the inside of the fork leg, and ensure the seal recess is cleaned properly.

10.20 A pair of new fork seals.

10.21 Slide the new seal over the stanchion.

10.22 Replace the damper rod.

10.23 Replace the coil spring.

10.24 Slide the stanchion into the leg …

10.25 … then push it in deep enough to refit the circlip. Once the circlip is in, ensure that it sits firmly inside the groove. Now replace the bottom bolt and dust cover.

10.26 Finally, fill with fork oil to the level recommended by the manufacturer. Most oil bottles have measurements on the side. If not, use a measuring jug.

Chapter 11
The rebuild

The rebuild can begin once you have the frame, swinging arm and stands repainted/resprayed. Before commencing, make sure that all nuts, bolts and washers are as clean as possible, or, if they are to be replaced, that you have replacements ready.

Some projects are rebuilt over a long period of time, due to the difficulty in finding parts, but you can still begin the rebuild, adding to the project when parts become available.

11.1 Raise the frame off the floor onto a solid platform, such as this bike lift. This will provide a good support when fitting the stand and swinging arm.

FRAME BUILD & REAR END

11.2 This particular model has a sump bash plate that must be fitted first.

11.3 Before fitting the swinging arm, apply plenty of grease to the swinging arm bushes ...

11.4 ...then insert them into the swinging arm.

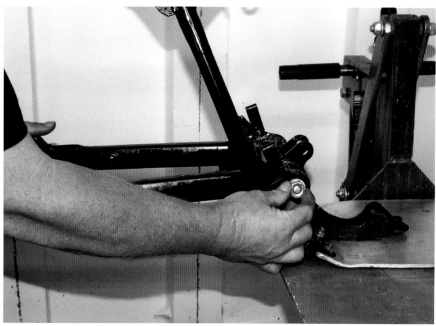

11.5 Fit the swinging arm by lightly tapping the bolt through with a rubber mallet. Make sure the large swinging arm bolt is tightened to the torque setting specified in the workshop manual. The swinging arm should now move freely, with no play at the bushes.

You will require a socket or spanner on both ends of the swinging arm bolt to prevent it from turning while tightening.

Now, while the frame is supported, fit the stand – lightly grease the eyes where the stand springs go through.

11.6 Next, fit both rear shock absorbers, ensuring that the rubbers are in good condition. If you don't have original dome nuts, you could use stainless steel ones instead. These nuts are always visible, and using stainless steel replacements will enhance the finished look. Some shock absorber units are fitted with bolts rather than nuts, in which case, use a nice stainless steel washer to hide the rubber bush.

11.7 Tighten all bolts/nuts on the top and bottom of the shock mounting.

11.10 ... the other two are hidden on the underside, behind the air filter housing.

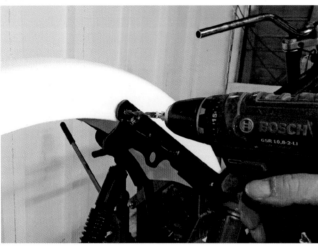

11.8 If you're fitting new plastic mudguards, most do not come with the holes pre drilled. Position the mudguard and drill though the fixing hole into the mudguard. Do this on the other side making sure it's exactly at the same height and level with the first hole that you drilled.

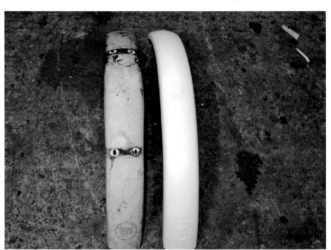

11.11 Check the fixing hole positions on the old mudguard.

11.9 The mudguards are secured by four bolts. Two are on the rear of the frame, as shown here ...

11.12 Position the bracket and drill all four holes, ensuring that they are even.

11.13 Depending on the model, the footrests can be fitted now, or after the rear brake lever. Don't forget to fit the return spring.

11.16 Hand-tighten spindle nuts until the chain has been fitted.

11.14 You can now fit the rear wheel. Make sure adjuster cams are in place.

11.17 Refit the rear wheel torque arm. Some designs require a split pit to be fitted.

11.15 Ensure that all spacers and washers are in the correct position.

11.18 Refit the rear brake arm; remember to replace the brake arm return spring.

11.19 Now you should have a setup that looks something like this.

FRONT END

11.20 When fitting the ball bearings, smear plenty of grease on the bearing carriers. Make sure the bearings are clean and greased before inserting them. This not only lubricates the bearings, but also prevents them from falling out while you're inserting the stem.

11.21 Apply plenty of grease to the carrier on the bottom yoke, too, and place the bearings on the carrier.

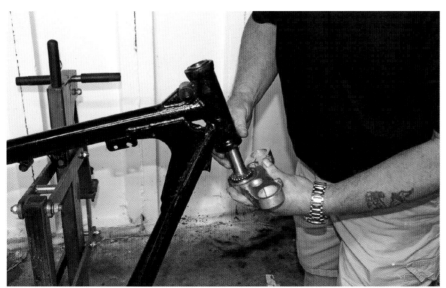

11.22 When inserting the steering stem make sure that no bearings fall out of the carriers. Slide it in carefully, trying not to let the top of the stem dislodge the bearings in the top yoke carrier.

11.23 Now fit the dust cover and nut. Hand-tighten for now.

If you're fitting taper roller bearings, you will have to remove the old ball bearing carriers. You will require a strong piece of steel rod, or similar, to tap them out. Fitting the taper bearings is quite easy, but you will need a piece of wood, placed over the bearing, that you gently tap in. Make sure you keep it square: if it begins to go in at an angle, it will get jammed – they're a very tight fit.

11.26 Some models have fork leg covers, and even headlamp brackets: fit these now before inserting the fork legs.

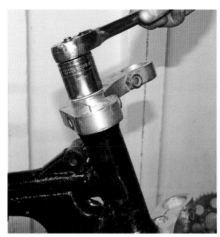

11.24 Support the stem from below until the dust cover and nut are fitted. Refit the top yoke, and tighten just enough so that no up and down movement is possible in the steering stem.

11.25 Some models have a top washer and pinch bolt, as seen here.

11.27 Slip the fork legs into the bottom yoke to the approximate height of the top yoke.

11.28 Tighten them according to the torque set out in your workshop manual.

Tighten the bolts on the top yoke, too.

11.29 If you have rubber gaiters, secure them with cable ties. Cut off the excess, and hide the end around the back of the forks so the cut is out of sight.

11.30 Now fit the handlebars. Ensure you line up the knurled part of the bars with the clamps. Set to the required position, then tighten the four bolts.

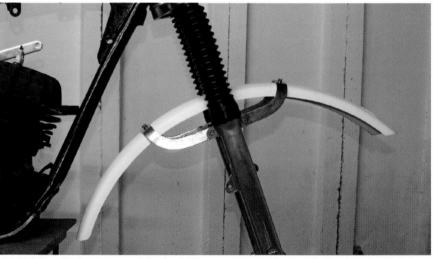

11.31 Now fit the front mudguard. There are usually four bolts for the fork leg.

11.32 There are two throttle types. If you have the classic one, as shown here, slide on the throttle twist grip. Note the hole for the throttle cable nipple.

11.33 Thread the cable nipples through, and slide them into the holes on the twist grip.

11.34 With quick action throttles, place the nipple in the holes, as before, and pull the cable around the pulley wheel. Fit the front brake lever, before sliding on the throttle control.

11.37 Tidy up the cabling. If you do not have the original cable ties, you can use tie wraps. (Original cable ties are usually available.)

11.35 Screw in the throttle cable adjuster, but leave it loose for now. This will need to be adjusted when the other end of the cable is fitted to the carburettors. Finally, firmly screw down the top of the throttle control.

11.38 Fit the clutch cable by placing the cable nipple in the slot on the underside of the clutch lever.

11.36 Now fit the clutch lever. Firmly screw down the holder with two screws that are located at the back. Set the levers at an angle you feel comfortable with.

11.39 Then line up the adjuster slots and push the cable into the slot.

11.40 Once the cable is in the slot, turn either of the adjusters so that the cable does not fall out. Screw the adjuster fully home. You will adjust the clutch properly later.

11.41 Slide on the handlebar grips at both ends.

FITTING THE FRONT WHEEL

11.42 If you have a speedometer, this must be fitted before re-fitting the front wheel. Make sure the speedometer drive is correctly located on the front wheel. There are two metal tabs that fit into the two slots on this model.

11.43 Re-fit the front brake drum into the front wheel hub.

11.44 Slide the front wheel spindle through the centre of the wheel, remembering to position the wheel spacers correctly.

11.45 Some forks have detachable bottom caps; keep these loose until the spindle is in the correct position. Then tighten all the caps – use spring lock washers.

11.46 Attach the front wheel torque arm at both ends.

11.47 If you haven't already done so, fit the front brake actuator arm.

11.50 Fit all engine mounting bolts.

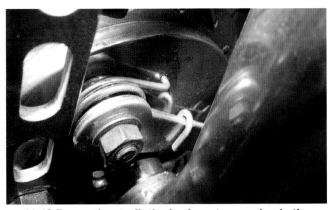

11.48 Remember to fit the brake return spring in the correct position; test it once it has been fitted. On this brake, the spring sits over the actuator arm and the other end slots into the brake hub.

11.51 This model also has an engine mounting above the cylinder head for extra strength.

11.49 With help, lift the engine into the frame; at the same time, ensure that the engine mounting bolt holes line up.

11.52 Refit the carburettor and tighten all hose clamps. Fit new ones, if necessary.

11.53 This model also has engine mounting stays that must be fitted after the carburettor is installed.

FITTING THE REAR WHEEL

Before re-fitting the rear wheel to the frame, its main components need to be reassembled correctly. These consist of the wheel, the sprocket carrier and the brake hub. The rear brakes on most classic motorcycles are drum brakes.

11.54 The inside of this brake drum has a light layer of rust which will need cleaning.

11.55 Using some 240 wet and dry paper, sand this back to a clean metal surface.

11.56 After a few minutes, the brake drum is ready for the brake hub.

11.57 The new brake shoes ready to be fitted.

11.58 The brake shoes here are showing signs of scoring, and are lightly glazed.

11.60 Slide the rear wheel spindle through the swinging arm and the rear hub, ensuring that all spacers are in the correct position, and that the rear wheel adjusters are fitted, too.

11.59 I would always recommend fitting new brake shoes. However, if these are not readily available, a light rub down with some wet and dry paper will remove the scoring and glaze, and should give a usable brake shoe.
Very important: Some brake material contains asbestos, and is dangerous if inhaled, so you must wear a dust mask.
The procedure should only be carried out if the brake shoe is not worn below the recommended wear limit.

11.61 Fit the wheel nut, with the washer.

11.62 On this model, it was necessary to connect the rear brake rod before bolting on the rear brake lever. This rod has a hooked end; most brake rods have a straight end that pushes through the lever, but then requires a washer and split pin, too.

11.63 Once the rod is in position behind the frame, you can fit the rear brake lever.

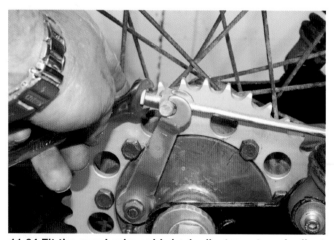

11.64 Fit the rear brake cable/rod adjuster nut, and adjust to the manufacturers' recommendation. On some models, a split pin will be inserted here, after adjustment has been completed.

11.65 Fit the rear wheel torque arm to the brake hub and swinging arm.

11.66 Now bolt on the foot pegs, ensuring that you use a return spring.

11.67 Bolt on the HT coil.

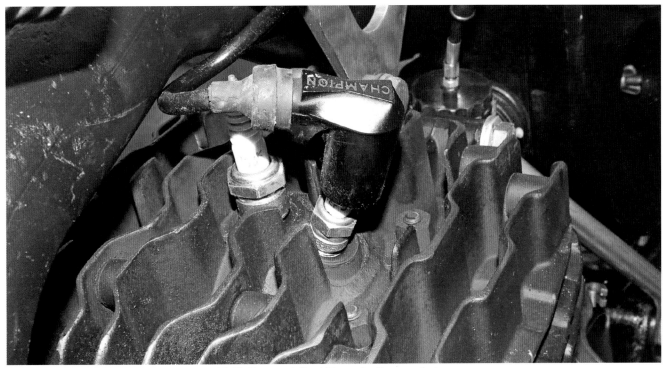

11.68 Connect the HT cap to the sparkplug.

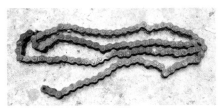

11.69 A typical old drive chain: no amount of soaking in oil is going to bring this back to a usable condition.

11.70 In most cases, the chain and sprockets will be worn, and in poor condition. I would certainly recommend fitting a new set. Try to get the correct sprocket sizes; this will ensure the gearing remains as intended by the manufacturer.

11.71 Place the chain on the rear sprocket, and feed it forwards towards the front sprocket.

11.72 Make sure that the engine is in neutral, pull the chain over the top of the sprocket and all the way back, until the two ends of the chain meet in the middle.

11.73 Now you will need the connecting link, which is in three parts.

11.74 Take the link and push through the two eyes in the end of the chain, completing the loop.

11.75 Place the other side of the link on the two link pins and push it back firmly, ensuring that the rear part of the link is pushed all the way through. You should see the slots in the pins at the ends.

11.76 Slide the split link onto the two slots as shown.

11.77 Making sure that the round end faces the direction of rotation, squeeze the end of the split link and one of the pins tightly, until the open end of the split link is forced over the second slot. Once the link has been fitted, it should look like this. You can see the split end has clipped firmly around the second pin.

11.78 Now adjust the rear wheel spindle until the wheel is straight within the swinging arm and the chain has the recommended tension. The spindle adjuster cams should be in the same position on both sides of the bike.

FITTING THE EXHAUST

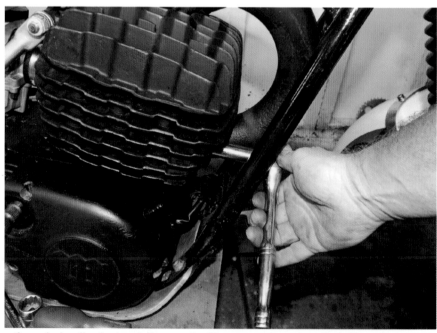

11.79 When fitting the exhaust system, always use new exhaust manifold gaskets. Use a little grease here on the gasket, as it will stop it dropping out when you are positioning the exhaust.

11.80 Bolt on the exhaust system. This is normally in two halves. The manifold bolts directly to the cylinder or cylinder head. Some models have a threaded collar instead. Be sure to fit a new exhaust gasket. Do not over-tighten the bolts/nuts/collar. This is a common location to find stripped threads on nuts or bolts. If, later, you find that the exhaust is blowing, and you feel you have tightened enough, you can add another exhaust manifold gasket to cure the problem. It is common for these bolts/nuts to come loose after a while, so keep an eye on them.

11.81 Now bolt on the silencer.

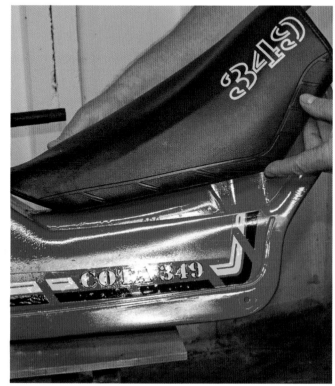

11.82 Re-fit the seat to the bike or, if you have an all-in-one seat tank unit as shown here, fit the seat to the unit.

11.83 Then re-fit the gearlever. Before tightening it, sit on the bike and make sure it is set at the correct angle.

11.84 Your motorcycle should now look something like this: very close to being finished, with only a few parts remaining to put back on.

11.85 Connect the fuel hose. Use hose clips to stop the fuel leaking. Although not essential, it is a good idea to fit an inline fuel filter, too.

11.86 Now connect the other end of the fuel pipe to the carburettor, and tighten the hose clamp.

With the main components now all fitted there will be a few smaller items that will now need to be added to complete the rebuild. These vary from model to model and should not be missed. They can be found in Chapter 12 Final preparation.

11.87 With all additional parts now fitted, the rebuild is complete.

VISIT VELOCE ON THE WEB – WWW.VELOCE.CO.UK
All current books • New book news • Special offers • Gift vouchers • Forum

129

Chapter 12
Final preparation

If you have followed the instructions detailed in previous chapters, and managed to get this far, you should now have a very respectable-looking off-road motorcycle. It may not be perfect – you may be awaiting some difficult-to-source part, and have had to continue, in the meantime, with a part that you'd really rather have changed – but you're almost there, and ready to set up your bike.

All the main components will now be in place, and the motorcycle almost ready to ride. There are a few settings and adjustments that are required at this stage. The detailed settings will be in the workshop manual, but many are common to most motorcycles, and these are detailed in this chapter. First,] though, check all the nuts, bolts and screws to make sure they are tight. It's very easy to have missed one, so check them now.

CABLES
Ensure that you have the correct cables for your motorcycle: pattern parts are fine, but cables from another make or model will not do. The cable length, the type of nipple and adjuster, can be quite different from one motorcycle to another.

All the cables on the motorcycle will have adjusters; some have one at each end of the cable. These help set the correct amount of tension or slack.

12.1 For the clutch cable, a good starting point to aim for is around 3-4mm (⅛in) of slack at the clutch lever. This ensures that it is fully engaged, and will not slip when riding. If the clutch cable is too tight, this slightly disengages the clutch, and will lead to slipping and early wear. Use the cable adjuster at the clutch lever end to set the slack, but don't unscrew it too much.

12.2 If you need to unscrew the cable adjuster this much at the clutch end, you will have to even out the amount of adjustment at the other end. If this is not possible, it's likely that the cable is the incorrect length. Only when you ride the motorcycle will you know if the clutch is adjusted properly, but if the clutch plates are in good condition, and with 3-4mm (⅛in) of slack at the clutch lever, I would say that the clutch is now adjusted correctly and should work fine.

12.3 Front brake cables usually have a setup similar to the clutch cable, with 3-4mm (⅛in) of slack at the lever – you should be able to pull back the lever by approximately that amount before brake actuation begins.

The throttle cable should be free moving and snap back under spring pressure, when released after opening to the full throttle position. The cable should have 1mm of free play at the carburettor end. If the cable has been routed correctly, this amount should not change when the handlebars are turned to full lock in either direction.

12.4 Both ends of the cables should be locked with the locking nuts, when the desired setting is reached.

12.6 On most motorcycles there are grease nipples. On this model each brake drum had a grease nipple, and there were two on the swinging arm. Make sure that you use a grease gun to apply grease to these areas. This will save wear on bushes, such as the swinging arm bush, and ultimately save you money.

12.5 The throttle cable adjuster is used to set the correct cable length, not to adjust engine speed.

TYRE PRESSURE AND TREAD

Check that the tyre pressures match those set by the manufacture, and that the tyres are not worn.

12.7 Set the tyre pressures appropriate for the competition. Trials pressures are generally set very low: around 8lb.

SPLIT PINS

Re-check that all castle nuts have split pins, and that every split pin has been bent open.

FIRST START-UP

So you now have your motorcycle back together, with everything bright and shiny. It looks great, just how you wanted it to. Unless it was a running bike when you bought it, you still haven't heard it run yet, though.

Now is the time to start it up for the first time.

Check the oil is to the correct level. Add fresh fuel, and, if the bike is a two-stroke model, check the two-stroke oil is mixed, too.

Is the sparkplug new? If not, is it clean and showing a good spark?

Make sure the engine kill switch is in the 'run' position, and turn the fuel tap to the 'on' position.

Check that the bike is not in gear, and employ the kickstart. Slightly open the throttle each time you try. It may take a few attempts, especially if the engine has been rebuilt, but, after two or three tries, it should at least fire. Once it fires and begins to run,

12.8 Set the choke to the 'on' position.

let it warm a little before opening the throttle further. If you open the throttle too early, the engine will flood and be more difficult to start next time.

After it has run for a minute or two, slowly open the throttle to bring up the revs: this will warm the engine quicker and get it to running temperature.

Does it sound okay? Keep an eye out for leaks (especially petrol). These must be plugged quickly. The most common leak at this stage is caused by the carburettors overflowing, because the valve in the float bowl has not seated properly, or a tiny piece of dirt is preventing it from closing. Try a gentle tap with a piece of wood on the float bowl; this often solves it and stops the leak. If there are no leaks, then great.

Does the engine settle if held at tickover speed? Most competition bikes do not have the engine set to run on tickover. (This is a safety measure: if a rider falls off the bike, the engine will cut out, even if the kill button is not used.) It often takes several attempts at setting the carburettors before the engine runs evenly without flat spots.

If the it does not misfire, runs okay, and will rev cleanly, it sounds like you've done a good job setting up the engine.

THE FIRST RIDE

If the bike is running well, you'll want to take it out for a trial ride.

Go through all the basic maintenance checks recommended

by the manufacturer: typically those set out below:

- Check the engine/gearbox oil level
- Check the two-stroke oil level
- Check the front and rear brakes are correctly adjusted
- Check the chain tension
- Lubricate the chain
- Check split pins are present
- Make sure you have enough fuel to complete your first ride
- Check the clutch lever play
- Check for leaks

12.9 Check and top up all oils. On this model, clutch and engine oil are separate; others may share oil.

For your first run, don't go too far: try the local club or track, if you can. There are usually teething troubles after a rebuild, and you don't want to break down miles from home.

A couple of laps around the track are enough; then come back and check that everything is okay. Slowly, you can increase your rides as you gain confidence that your newly rebuilt bike is not going to break down on you.

If the engine has been rebuilt, remember to run it in as recommended by the manufacturer. Everything will be new and tight, and will need some gentle running before you can use the full rev range.

Remember, after a short running-in period, the cylinder head bolts and exhaust bolts usually need to be torqued again (check your workshop manual). Once this has been done, just keep an eye on fluid levels and you've finished!

Chapter 13
Pre '65 competition

My teenage memories centre on trials and scramble events in Essex, England in the 1970s. My father and I were regular attendees. At the time, the older British machines were competing in the same classes with newer Spanish and Japanese models. Like any teenager, I was interested in the most modern bikes of the time: Suzukis, Yamahas, Bultacos, Maicos and the like – the lighter weight two-stroke models; while my father,

having raced scramblers himself as a youngster, was far more interested in the older machines: BSAs, Triumphs and Nortons. As time passed, the older bikes were becoming more and more of a rarity in these events: I remember one meeting where just one four-stroke scrambler competed – a shame, as they were all good examples of solid British machines, which, until then, had been the backbone of all motorcycling.

Thankfully, this situation did not last: enthusiasts began to form small clubs and hold specific events for these older models. Soon, the older machines were given their own class, and Pre '65 was born. Within a few years, this classic form of competition had spread far and wide, and, nowadays, there is an excellent choice of Pre '65 events for both scrambling (motocross) and trials, with a sizeable following worldwide.

13.1 You'd be forgiven for thinking that this was a scene from the 1960s, but no: this scramble club runs regular events throughout the year, and the photo was taken at a wonderful farm location in Essex, England, in 2016. With over 100 entrants, it's clear to me that these Pre '65 competition bikes aren't collecting dust in the back of an old shed, but competing, full on, just as they did years ago. Classic racing is alive and well. In fact, at this meeting, there were riders who were still racing the same motorcycle that they were racing 40 years ago.

13.2 Up goes the front wheel, and they're off!

13.3 These guys didn't just turn up to make up the numbers: they were full throttle as soon as the starting flag was dropped, and were determined to compete well.

13.4 We even had sidecar combinations racing. This Norton Wasp outfit uses the engine from a Norton Commando motorcycle (albeit heavily tuned). It has also had disk brakes fitted to improve the braking.

13.5 The passenger is almost touching the ground trying to keep the outfit upright.

13.6 We have lift-off: this pair stole the show, and finished a good distance ahead of the competition.

13.8 There were many 'specials' built by owners, usually to match the better frames with the more desirable engines of the day. This is a prime example, with a Triumph engine in a BSA frame.

13.7 Arguably top of the list in Pre '65 motocross: the BSA B50 MX, a superbly powerful model that is still the envy of new enthusiasts today.

13.9 An event in Lincolnshire, England: the Poacher Pre '65 Trials Club hold regular meetings throughout the year. I came across this wonderful Matchless trials bike, looking very much as it did back in the old days. Note the coloured markers: each one indicating a different route of varying difficulty through the same trials section.

13.10 This lovely little BSA Bantam is modified to cope with the trials sections that it faces during a typical event today. Note the high ground clearance, the long travel rear shocks, and the masterpiece of an exhaust pipe.

13.11 This Royal Enfield is a very nice example of a Pre '65 trials bike.

13.12 A rider tackling a steep bank during a Pre '65 trial. Note the coloured markers that guide the rider through different routes that vary in difficulty.

Chapter 14
Twinshock competition

Twinshock competition came about much in the same way as Pre '65 competition. With the introduction of monoshock machines, twinshock models could not compete; this was true in trials or motocross. Soon, serious competitors upgraded to monoshock models; and twinshocks looked destined for the scrap heap, before a new twinshock class was introduced.

While Pre '65 models did have twin shock absorbers, the 'twinshock' period is associated more with the mid/late '70s and early '80s, before Yamaha heralded in the new monoshock machines with the YZ 250, the first production monoshock motocross bike, in 1975.

Suzuki also produced the RL250 trials bike, which, in its original form, didn't prove to be as

14.1 The Yamaha TY175 proved to be a very popular choice for twinshock trials; known for its agility and bullet proof reliability, it is still a popular choice today. (Courtesy Robbie Rogers)

competitive as hoped. 50 were sent to Beamish Motors in England, and were modified so successfully that Beamish offered to buy all stock

from Suzuki. Beamish went on to sell 1200, which also included a 325cc model. It produced the only dedicated sidecar outfit, too.

14.2 A 1976 Suzuki RM250 twinshock scrambler, in great condition and looking brand new. Suzuki would continue to use the twinshock setup for another five years. (Courtesy Paul Phillips)

14.3 A very smart Suzuki Beamish trials outfit.

14.4 Early twinshocks were practically upright, such as here, in the Bultaco Pursang.

I cannot finish this book without a mention to all the fabulous volunteers who turn up, rain or shine, and keep these sports, classic or otherwise, going. There's a huge amount of organisation to be done before any event can take place. Without their generosity with their time, there would be no sport of this kind. From finding landowners willing to loan their land for a day or weekend, to the people acting as safety marshals – one on every bend – or as a spotter in a trials event, these tasks are all carried out by volunteers, and to them, we owe our thanks.

14.5 An observer volunteer marking scores at a trials event, watching for a foot down (dab), a complete halt, or a stall; all gain points. The competitor with the lowest points wins.

14.6 The starter, waiting to see the green all-clear flag from every other marshal, before he can start the race.

14.7 The finish flag, signalling the end of the race; the end of a great day's racing.

Also from Veloce Publishing ...

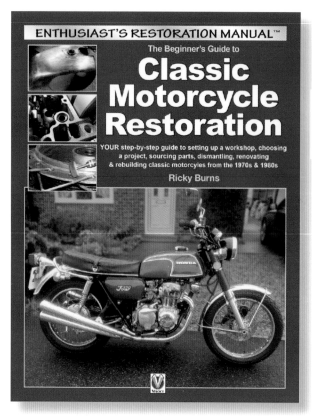

Seasoned motorcycle restorer Ricky Burns goes through each of the stages of a real-life restoration. From choosing a project, setting up a workshop, and preparing a bike, to sourcing parts, dismantling, restoring and renovating, this book is the perfect guide for the classic motorcycle restorer.

ISBN: 978-1-845846-44-2
Paperback • 27x20.7cm • £30* UK/$49.95* USA
• 144 pages • 594 pictures

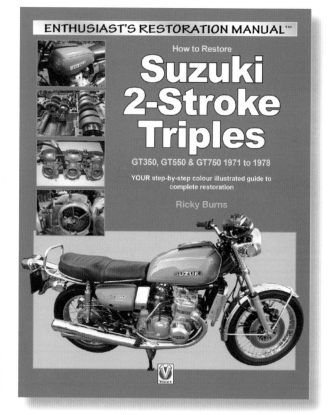

Whether it be an entry level GT380, or a ground-breaking water-cooled GT750, this step-by-step full restoration guide covers it, from dismantling, sourcing parts, spraying and decals, to polishing, safe set-up and general maintenance. Even riding safely and storage are covered, making this a must-have guide for all Suzuki Triple enthusiasts.

ISBN: 978-1-845848-20-0
Paperback • 27x20.7cm • £35* UK/$59.95* USA
• 176 pages • 586 colour pictures

For more info on Veloce titles, visit our website at www.veloce.co.uk • email: info@veloce.co.uk • Tel: +44(0)1305 260068
* prices subject to change, p&p extra

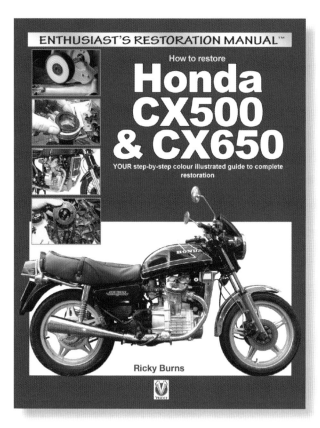

This book provides a step-by-step guide to a full restoration of the Honda CX500 & CX650. From dismantling, sourcing and restoring parts, to spray painting, decals and polishing. From the rebuild itself, to general maintenance and riding safety, this is the only restoration manual you'll need.

ISBN: 978-1-845847-73-9
Paperback • 27x20.7cm • £35* UK/$59.95* USA • 176 pages
• 759 colour pictures

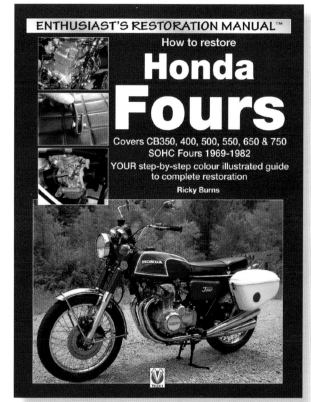

This book gives enthusiasts of the single overhead camshaft Honda Four a step-by-step guide to a full restoration. Whether it be the small but luxurious CB350/4 right through to the groundbreaking CB750/4. This guide covers dismantling the motorcycle and its components, restoring and sourcing parts, paint spraying, decals and polishing. The chapters cover, Engine, frame, forks, fuel, exhaust, seat, brakes, tyres, electrics, up to the rebuild and on to safe setup and general maintenance and finally onto riding safely and storage.

ISBN: 978-1-845847-46-3
Paperback • 27x20.7cm • £35* UK/$59.95* USA
• 176 pages • 682 colour pictures

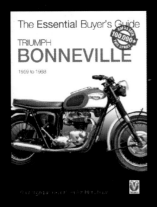
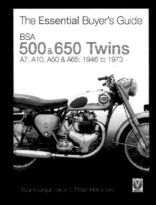

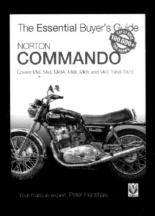
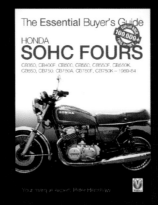

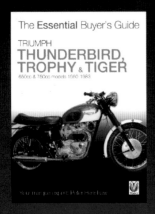

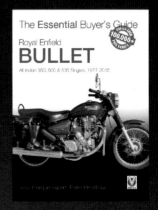

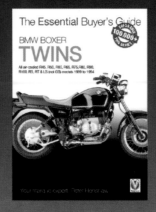

Heroes of 1960s Motorcycle Sport

Off-Road Giants!

Andy Westlake

Volume 1, reprinted as a paperback after a four year gap! A fascinating and nostalgic compilation of rider profiles written over a three year period, that originally appeared in *Classic Motorcycle* magazine, now accompanied by a new set of over 100 photographs. This book beautifully captures a much-loved time in motorsport.

ISBN: 978-1-845848-35-4
Paperback • 25x20.7cm • £25* UK/$49.95* USA • 128 pages
• 115 b&w pictures

Heroes of 1960s Motorcycle Sport

Off-Road Giants!

Volume 2

Andy Westlake

Volume 2 includes personal interviews with some of the greats of off-road motorcycling from the 1950s, 1960s and 1970s, along with some stunning period photographs that paint a wonderful picture of what motorcycling was about in this golden era.

ISBN: 978-1-845843-23-6
Hardback • 25x20.7cm • £19.99* UK/$39.95* USA •
128 pages • 123 b&w pictures

Volume 3 details some of the greats of the scrambling world – Dave Bickers, John Banks, Rob Taylor – and others not, perhaps, quite so well known. From the hard-riding Devon farmer John Trible, Gloucester ace Tommy Barker, and Six Days trials star Eric Chilton, to the last ever interview with Olga Kevelos, a true star.

ISBN: 978-1-845847-45-6
Hardback • 25x20.7cm • £25* UK/$45* USA
• 128 pages • 124 b&w pictures

Off-Road Giants!

Volume 3

Andy Westlake

For more info on Veloce titles, visit our website at www.veloce.co.uk
• email: info@veloce.co.uk • Tel: +44(0)1305 260068
* prices subject to change, p&p extra

Index